AN APPENDIX

TO

THE STATE

OF THE

PROTESTANT RELIGION

IN GERMANY;'

BEING

A REPLY

TO THE GERMAN CRITIQUES ON THAT WORK.

BY

HUGH JAMES ROSE, B.D.

LONDON:

PRINTED FOR C. & J. RIVINGTON,

ST. PAUL'S CHURCH-YARD, AND WATERLOO-PLACE, PALL-MALL;

AND J. & J. J DEIGHTON, CAMBRIDGE.

1828.

LONDON :

PRINTED BY R. GILBERT,

ST. JOHN'S SQUARE.

ERRATA.

Page 7. line 8. for *churches* read *church.*
22. — 14. for *other* read *these.*
34. — 13. for *dialects* read *dialectics.*
36. — 15. for *as* read *in.*
39. — 24. insert comma after *true.*
41. — 8. for *then* read *there.*
45. — 13. for *hypothesis* read *hypotheses.*
65. last line, put reference to a note.
67. — 12. ditto.
73. — 2. for *where* read *whether.*
77. — 15. after *revelation* insert *only.*
80. — 13. for *effected* read *affected.*
95. — 26. for *more* read *mere.*
114. — 31. for *Pfaff* read *Walch.* The copy of this book from which I had derived the particulars given in the note, has since arrived. Its title is 'Breviarium Theologiæ Symbol. Eccles. Lutheranæ, Götting. 1765.' The father's work is 'Introductio in libros Symbolicos.'
124. line 3. I have not given the title of this pamphlet correctly. It is 'Ueber das Liturgische Recht Evangelischer Landesfürsten, ein theologisches bedenken von Pacificus Sincerus.' This was printed at Göttingen, but widely circulated in Prussia.
135. note. I now believe, that the article alluded to, is the work of Professor Stapfer, though I have no proof of it.
137. — 36. for *system* read *systems.*
140. — 12. for *Danb* read *Daub.*
154. — 4. after *viz.* dele *by.*
157. — 30. after *The doctrine* insert *of the Trinity.*
160. — 6 and 9. read *Zachariah.*

ADVERTISEMENT.

———

Thε following pages contain a reply * to various writers, who have objected to my statements respecting Protestantism in Germany. I have made that reply as short as possible, not only for the reader's sake, but for my own. For the class of writers opposed to me is one, with which they, who know them, desire to have as little commerce as possible. I may perhaps be thought to speak in bitterness, and I therefore prefer giving the character of the German Rationalists as controversialists, drawn by one of their own countrymen, the excellent and lamented Staüdlin, in his ' Geschichte des Rationalismus und Supernaturalismus,' (Göttingen, 1826), a work of high interest, of which I heartily

---

* The substance of the answers to the translators of my Sermons, and to Dr. Bretschneider, has already appeared in the ' Christian Remembrancer.'

hope to see a translation, as the best possible confirmation of all I have said. In speaking of the author of a book called ' Briefe über den Rationalismus,' who, though he goes the full length of Rationalism, is remarkable for the moderation and the gentlemanlike tone in which he writes, and for the respect which he shows to the opinions and feelings of those who differ from him, Staüdlin observes, that ' many other Rationalists of our day, on the contrary, write with ill-breeding, rudeness, violence, presumption, and intolerance, that they scatter terms of abuse, and treat all who differ from them with sneers and contempt, as irrational and ignorant creatures, though they exhibit themselves a very low degree of philosophy and learning. *One cannot but be ashamed of entering into a controversy with them.*' (P. 323.) It is, indeed, sufficiently humiliating to have any thing to do with writers who cannot treat the greatest and most momentous questions, without raising a cry of knavery or folly against all who differ from them. My reason for noticing them is simply this. Their character is very little known in this country; and, however reluctant I may

be to make such an accusation, my readers will
see that some of them have had unsparing recourse to one art of controversy of great service
in defeating an adversary, while he who uses it
can maintain his own credit, I mean, the un-
blushing assertion of direct falsehoods. I feel
it, therefore, a duty to those who have been interested in the statements I have made, to shew
that their credit is not shaken by any thing
which my adversaries have advanced.

Let me add, that in what I have now said,
I do not mean to make any complaint of the
manner in which these persons have spoken of
me; but to explain why I think it sufficient to
notice their arguments and assertions, and then
to drop all further mention of them. On the
contrary, I can say, with great truth, that all
which they have already said, and all which
they may say hereafter, is a matter of the most
entire indifference to me. Where one is un-
fortunate enough to be engaged in controversy
with adversaries who lay aside the courtesy of
gentlemen, and condescend to abuse and per-
sonality, it is impossible to feel any pain at their

resentment, or any regret at their degrading themselves by violence and falsehood.

My readers may be interested in knowing, that a violent controversy with respect to Rationalism sprung up at Leipsic, in the course of last autumn, in consequence of an inaugural dissertation by Professor Hahn, who has been called to Leipsic from Königsberg, and who is steadily opposed to the views of the Rationalists. Of this controversy I shall give an account in the second edition of my Sermons, which will shortly appear.

In conclusion, I must state that I have been informed that the well-known Göttingen Journal, the ' Gelehrte Anzeigen,' contained a notice of my work ; but that two gentlemen who have kindly undertaken to examine the numbers of that Journal for me, have been unable to find it. I mention this, lest it should be imagined that I have sought to avoid taking notice of any particular attack.

HORSHAM,
February 23, 1828.

CONTENTS.

I. GENERAL REMARKS.

BEFORE noticing any particular reply to my statements respecting Protestantism in Germany, I am desirous of making a few general remarks on them all.

The object of my work was to shew that certain opinions, entirely at variance with what is commonly considered as Christianity in England, have been widely held and taught in Germany, and that the influence they attained is mainly attributable to certain deficiencies in the Constitution of the German Churches. The statements which I made, undoubtedly represented a very singular state of things; and the inferences to which they led are assuredly of very considerable importance. As several German writers have undertaken to destroy the credit of my work, I am anxious to afford the English reader an opportunity of judging between my antagonists and myself; and of ascertaining, (1.) Whether I have *endeavoured* to represent things fairly; and (2.) whether I have succeeded in doing so, or in other words, whether my account may be relied on.

To the English Reader then I would beg to present the following brief view of the case.

My principal adversaries admit that I have *endeavoured* to write fairly, but they accuse me of having been misled by others, of ignorance and of exaggeration. To the first of these accusations I beg to put in here a distinct and positive denial, and to say, that I have received no assistance whatever. The correctness or incorrectness of my statements is wholly due to myself. With respect to the charges of ignorance and exaggeration, I must refer the reader to the following pages for my defence. But I must add here, what may perhaps be still more satisfactory to many persons, and what could not be adduced in reply to any specific charges, viz. the testimonies of other writers to the truth of the statements I have made. It will then be easy for others to judge, whether in accusing a vast portion of the German Protestant divines of holding opinions which degrade Christianity from a divine to a human institution, I went beyond the truth.

First, I will adduce the words of Reinhard, one

of those admirable and venerable men who in an apostate age adhered firmly, though always mildly, to the degraded and contemned doctrines of Christianity.

'I became,' says he, 'a Preacher at a time when our innovating theologians had arrived at making the Christian system so simple and so easy to comprehend, that *it was nothing more than pure Deism.* At this epoch, *whoever aspired to reputation, or to the eulogies of the journals, must, as an almost indispensable condition, have attacked the authenticity of some book of Scripture, or the truth of some point of doctrine.* He who dared to present himself in public without paying his tribute *to the spirit of the age,* had no other reception to expect than contempt and ridicule—you know that I experienced how incomprehensible my attachment to old ideas was judged to be, and with what injustice, harshness, and bitterness, the journalists spoke of it. One indeed thought it right ᵗₒ collect the bitterest of these reproaches and to form them into a little volume *.' Reinhard then goes on to state, that he never said a word in his own defence, but that *his friends* endeavoured to

* Neueste Protestantische bekenntnisse uber Sectengeist und kanzel-krieg, veranlasst durch die Reinhardische Reformationspredigt von 1800, gesammelt von Wilhelm Köster.

excuse him, by saying ' that it was not from ignorance that he adhered to *a superannuated faith*—
that circumstances probably compelled him (for
there could be no doubt that he *was perfectly convinced of the truth of the new opinions—what man
of sense could think otherwise?*) or that perhaps
he thought that a teacher of religion was bound
to teach what was presented to him.'   After noticing how painful such a defence was to one who
loved truth above all things, he explains how
he arrived at a belief in orthodox Christianity.
He observes, that the only consistent opinions are
pure Deism, and a full belief in Christianity as a
divine Revelation; that a mixture which allows
a sort of joint and equal reign of Reason and the
Word of God can only lead to confusion, and to a
want of clear views and fixed principles.   He then
adds, ' This middle road appeared to me to be that
taken by most of the theologians who were at work
to purify Christianity. I say *by most;* for an atten-
tive observer saw clearly that there were men among
them who perfectly knew to what their opinions
tended, in a word, *true Deists,* who found it more
prudent not to announce their real character, who
in the bottom of their hearts rejected all positive
religion without publicly attacking it. But in fact
the greatest number of innovating theologians did
not know what they wished, and did not understand

to what their efforts led. They thought they had done a great service to truth in rejecting first one and then another doctrine of the old system, while they retained others, which on the same grounds they ought to have rejected. Thus was introduced into dogmatic theology a vacillation which deprived it of *all character of a system*. The greater part of these people did not know where they were ; detached from the old system where Scripture decided every thing, but not having yet gained resolution to withdraw themselves wholly from its authority and to recognize only that of reason, these theologians established a sort of absurd compromise between the two. Sometimes they sought to satisfy reason at the expense of Scripture, sometimes they made it stoop to tolerate certain things too clearly taught to be denied. This was a negociation in which the parties alternately triumphed, as the negociator might chance to aspire to the reputation of Critic or Philosopher, and as his particular situation gave him more or less liberty. Can one be angry with Lessing for taking every occasion to laugh at this miserable system of the New Teachers, for expressing aloud his disgust at it, and his preference for the ancient orthodoxy *.'

* The above passage is a translation of the French translation

It is true that it may be replied, that Reinhard
is of a different opinion from the Rationalists.
But on the one hand Reinhard was proverbial for
his freedom from all violence; on the other, neither
he nor a far more violent person could have any
desire to exaggerate *the extent* of opinions which
they disapprove.

Staüdlin in his latest work, ' the History of
Rationalism and Supernaturalism,' in speaking of
the eighteenth century, says, that ' Rationalism
made greater strides during this period than it had
ever done before, especially in Germany, and in
the Protestant Church,' and that it is ' extraordinary and difficult to explain how Rationalism

---

of a work of Reinhard's called, in German, Geständnisse seine
predigten und seine bildung zum prediger betreffend ; in French,
Lettres de F. V. Reinhard sur ses études et sa carrière de Pré-
dicateur, Paris, 1816.   It is translated by M. Monod, the well-
known Protestant Minister at Paris, and there is an appendix
of some interest by Mr. Stapfer.—Let me take this occasion of
recommending a most admirable work of Reinhard called, Ver-
such über den Plan, den der stifter uns. Religion zum besten der
Menschheit entworfen. 8vo. Wittemberg, 1798. It is translated
by M. Dumas under the title, Essai sur le Plan formé par le
Fondateur de la Réligion Chrétienne pour le bonheur du genre
humain. Dresden, 1799.   It is an admirable refutation of the
fancy that Christianity is only a sort of re-edition of more ancient
wisdom and morals.

should have gained so great a preponderance, and so wide an extension among Christians *.'

I. A. H. Tittman, in the preface to his Pragmatische Geschichte, p. 8, 9, in which he gives an account of the Rationalist opinions (agreeing *in its facts* with mine, and attempting to account for 'the existing state of theology and religion') states, perhaps truly, that it is not quite fair to charge the persons of the present day with the whole of the evil, part of which arises from preceding opinions and circumstances over which they had no controul. 'Unless I err,' says he, ' their preceding circumstances are forgotten, in judging of the present state of theological matters; and the blame of all that disorder and confusion *which are undeniable*, is laid on our contemporaries.' Are such phrases as ' the existing state of religion and theology,' and ' the disorder and confusion which are undeniable,' intended to describe the movements of a small and inconsiderable party? Hear the same writer again, Ch. 24. p. 306. He is speaking of the discarding of the symbolical books. ' Through this giving up, one might rather say, through this disregard of considerations before esteemed so weighty, things went so far, that by

* P. 282.

degrees, the notion of a fixed and enduring view
of doctrine gave way to the most entire freedom
of enquiry; and the greatest part of the divines
of this period held themselves as justified in following simply, without any regard to external
circumstances, the views presented by the exposition of Scripture through history, philosophy,
and knowledge of languages.' And again, Ch. 26.
p. 326. he speaks of ' the most suspicious appear-
ances of this period (the last half of the eighteenth
century) viz. the tendency by degrees to get rid
of the view of Christianity which represents it a
peculiar revelation, and to explain as non-essen-
tials, and unnecessary for the present day, certain
doctrines peculiar to it.'

But let us turn to other quarters: What says
Göthe? He says plainly, that when he left Leipsic
in 1768, ' the Christian Religion in Germany
was fluctuating between its own constitution
founded on historical traditions as well as positive
laws, and *pure Deism*.' (Translation of Göthe's Life,
vol. i. p. 247.) But what say others, Planke for example, and Lehmann, and Boll, and Beckendorf,
and the historian Müller? It is impossible in the
limits of a pamphlet to adduce the opinions of all
these persons, but at a more convenient opportunity I will show, what I can now only assert, that

these persons speak of the state of the Protestant Religion in even stronger terms than I have done, and that some of them declare unreservedly that there are indeed Churches, but no longer any Church in Germany.

But again, I am accused of speaking with too much violence on the state of Rationalist theology. I am well aware that no cause however righteous, no ground of complaint however just, can afford a pretext for violence; and if any intemperance of language (I am not aware of it) has mixed itself in the expression of my feelings on this important subject, I beg here to declare my sincere and unfeigned regret for it. But on this point too I deem it important to show that my estimate of the perniciousness of the doctrines, and the mischief they have effected, is not exaggerated. I might here adduce numberless witnesses; but I shall content myself with one, that of Tittmann of Dresden, because his character must be known to many of my readers who are not acquainted with German, by his excellent Latin commentary on St. John's Gospel.

In the Preface to that work, after a most able exposure of the system of historical interpretation, he goes on to characterise it as follows:

' What is the interpretation of the Scriptures if
it relies not on words, but things, not on the assistance of languages, but on the decrees of reason, that is, of modern philosophy ?   What is all
religion, what the knowledge of divine things,
what are faith and hope placed in Christ, what is
all Christianity, if human reason and philosophy is the only fountain of divine wisdom and
the supreme judge in the matter of religion ?
What is the doctrine of Christ and the Apostles
more than some philosophical system ?   But what
then, I pray you, is, to deny, to blaspheme Jesus
the Lord, to render his divine mission doubtful,
nay vain and useless, to impugn his doctrine, to
disfigure it shamefully, to attack it, to expose it
to ridicule, and if possible, to suppress it, to remove all Christianity out of religion, and to bound
religion within the narrow limits of reason alone,
to deride miracles, and hold them up to derision,
to accuse them as vain, to bring them into disre-
pute, to torture sacred Scripture into seeming
agreement with the fancies of human wisdom, to
alloy it with human conjectures, to bring it into
contempt, and to break down its divine authority,
to undermine, to shake, to overthrow utterly the
foundations of Christian faith ?   What else can be
the event than this, as all history, a most weighty
witness in this matter informs us, namely, that

when sacred Scripture, its grammatical interpretation and a sound knowledge of languages are, as it were, despised and banished, all religion should be contemned, shaken, corrupted, troubled, undermined, utterly overturned, and should be entirely removed and reduced to natural religion; or that it should end in a mystical theology, than which nothing was ever more pernicious to the Christian doctrine, and be converted into an empty Μυθολογία, or even into a poetical system, hiding every thing in figures and fictions, to which latter system not a few of the sacred orators and theologians of our time seem chiefly inclined, &c. &c.'

But there is still one other consideration which I am desirous to submit to the English Reader. Putting aside all notice of particular accusations of inaccuracy which are answered in the following pages in detail, let me enquire, what is the answer which has been given to the accusations I have produced, viz. that for some years the German Protestant Churches have not been bound by any rule of faith; and that, in consequence, a very large and influential body of Clergy have openly professed and taught doctrines which more or less tend to deprive Christianity of its character as an immediate Revelation? I say, with truth,

that I find no other answer than this—that Theology, like other sciences, must make progress—
that enquiry cannot be stopped—that it is better
to have learned and enquiring men as divines,
even though their opinions differ from those laid
down in the symbolical books, than mere men of
form—that Scripture, interpreted as every one
can, is a sufficient rule of faith—and that the
Church of England with all its thirty-nine Articles is in a very bad state. This is the sum
of the reply of one of my two principal opponents. The other repeats these arguments and
adds to them this only—that I am wrong in de-
scribing the Rationalists as one party, for that in
fact there are four classes of them; the three first
of which, according to the writer's own admission, go to the full lengths which I have stated;
and the fourth, which he declares to be the largest,
and which he considers as the very perfection of
Christianity, ' regards the Bible and Christianity
as a Divine Revelation in a higher sense than the
Rationalists, inasmuch as they admit a revealing
energy of God, distinguishable from his general
Providence; carefully discriminate the periods of
this divine communication; ground the divinity of
Christianity more on its internal evidence than on
its miracles; but chiefly draw a distinction between Scripture-doctrines and Church-creeds;

reform the latter by the decisions of the divine word; but as regards the relation between reason and Revelation, maintain that it is the province of reason to scrutinize Revelation, which must not contain any thing *contrary to reason,* though it contain much that *is above it.*' Now if I were disposed to cavil, I might certainly ask whether *Rationalism* could be more distinctly represented than in this creed, which professes to reject it? Who is a true Rationalist, but he who thinks that it is the business of reason to scrutinize *what is confessed to be Revelation,* or who acknowledges it to be a Revelation, *only* by its accordance with what his reason judges to be true? But this is a matter of little importance; I am desirous rather to point out the singularity of this creed as the creed of Christians. If they who hold it have *not* rejected the positive doctrines of Christianity, why not say so simply and distinctly, and thus at once put me to silence and to shame? It is in vain to hope that men can be deceived by a pretended dislike to Church systems and scholastic definitions and distinctions. We desire to know this and this only. Do the professors of this creed believe in the Divinity of the Saviour, in the justification of man through the Saviour's sacrifice, and in his sanctification by the Spirit? If they *do* believe in these doctrines, I repeat it, the bare

statement of that belief will put me to confusion;
if they do not believe them, why not equally avow
their creed, and why complain of me for saying
that they do not believe doctrines which they consider as neither Christian nor Scriptural? For
this is the head and front of my offending.

If any thing more were necessary to shew what
the opinions, so studiously held back, are, or
rather what they are not, that farther information
would be afforded by the simple fact, that there
has been and still is a party of admirable and
learned men in Germany, (thank God, it is an in-
creasing one) which has always held the opinions
usually called orthodox, and that these persons
are *never named nor alluded to* in this studied enumeration. Their existence is as studiously passed
over by my antagonist, as the nature of those
opinions, which he considers as pre-eminently
Christian. These things speak for themselves;
they speak indeed far more strongly than could
any statement of mine. I can only wonder that
they who are guilty of such disingenuousness
should be blind to the unfavourable impressions
towards their cause which it must produce.

II. TRANSLATION OF THE SERMONS INTO GERMAN.

===

THIS translation appeared at the Leipsic Spring-fair in 1826. It is anonymous, but the Theologisches Literatur-blatt, an appendix to the Allgemeine Kirchen-Zeitung (for Friday, Dec. 15, 1826.) states that it is done by 'Herr Prediger Rosenmüller.' Whether this gentleman is the author of the Commentary on the Old Testament, or any relation of his, I have no means of determining. He did not rely on his own strength for my extermination, but called in *four* friends to his aid, who sign their remarks with the most laudable precision, as First Annotator, Second Annotator, &c. The preface is filled with abuse of the Church of England, and collaudations of the warmer devotion of the Wesleyan Methodists. The notes in general contain arguments (neither new nor well put) in favour of Rationalism. I have no intention of noticing these, but willingly leave to each Annotator the meed of praise due

to him for his ingenuity. 'Et vitula tu dignus,
et hic.' I only regret to observe, that these gentlemen do not seem to have obtained in Germany
the praise of discretion for their zeal in transla-
ting my work and confuting me. On the contrary, Dr. Bretschneider says very plainly, that
they would have shewn much more wisdom in
leaving the work untranslated and hushing the
whole matter up. 'The statements I have made,'
he says, 'may now very possibly fall into the
hands of German statesmen and ministers, and
prejudice the interests of the Rationalist party!
while, if Mr. Preacher Rosenmüller, and his
friends had been quiet, these statesmen might have
known nothing of the matter!' I condole with
Mr. Rosenmüller and his four Annotators very
heartily on this waste of their time and labour.

My concern with them is a very brief one.
They have only impeached my accuracy in two
cases, and when I have shown how their impeach-
ment in those two cases is conducted, I need not
add, that if they had produced an hundred more
accusations, I should hold myself perfectly ab-
solved from the task of answering them.

Their first charge is as follows: I have said
(p. 159, 160,) that 'with regard to the prophe-

cies, it will be seen from Rosenmüller's Proem to the third volume of his Commentary on Isaiah, that he considers that book as made up by one writer out of the minor works of several.' The third Annotator has here added the following note :—'Rosenmüller says exactly the contrary. (Isaiah, Part iii. p. 6, 2d Edit. *) Contineri hoc libro *non* diversa plurium auctorum scripta minora in unum syntagma conjuncta, sed ab uno eodemque Scriptore integrum librum proficisci, illud arguit,' &c. No contradiction certainly can apparently be more direct; yet it is produced by a mere dishonest trick. First of all, I will shew that I have stated Rosenmüller's opinion quite justly, and this will be clear from the following quotations from the Commentary on Isaiah, Part III. Vol. I. p. 4. 'Quum autem omnia quæ in hoc volumine continentur vaticinia, in unum corpus colligerentur, *cui Jesaiæ, celebris olim vatis, nomen præfigere visum esset,* illi qui eo negocio fungebantur, oraculum hocce (the first in order) grave illud et generalioris argumenti in

---

* That Rosenmüller has, in a later edition of his Commentary, renounced many of his offensive opinions, is a fact which I have mentioned elsewhere. I have not seen this later edition of the Commentary on Isaiah. Nor can any change in his opinions affect the matter in question.—The passage referred to, stands in the second edition.

fronte libri possuerunt *,' &c. Again (p. 9.) ' Je-
saiana tamen oracula a manibus serioribus varie
esse interpolata, *imo integris Carminibus alienis,*
hic illic insertis adaucta, accuratior singularium
hujus libri partium disquisitio docebit.' It will
not be worth while to refer to more than a few
instances of what we learn from this accurate examination. The first four verses of chap. ii. are
probably older than Isaiah's time, according to
Rosenmüller. On chap. xxi. he says, that the
pretended prophecy of the fall of Babylon contained in it, was written at the time of that fall,
and not in the age of Isaiah; and in the preface
to chap. xxiii. he says exactly the same as to the
prophecy of the fall of Tyre, adding, that many
words used there, shew that this part is later than
the time of Isaiah. It now remains to account

---

* This opinion is even more explicitly stated in p. 459 of the
same volume, where Rosenmüller states his belief that chap. xiii.
is the work of an age later than that of Isaiah, adding, ' At Jesaiæ
nomen Carmen nostrum in fronte gerit? Quasi vero non consta-
ret, esse tam *in hoc nostro, cui a Jesaia est nomen, vaticiniorum
corpore,* quam in aliis vaticiniorum collectionibus, plura capita,
quibus ab illis, qui hos libros conscripserunt *et in unum college-
runt,* falsum scriptoris nomen esset præpositum.' Had I referred
to these places, my dishonest adversary could not have taken
advantage of me. But, in fact, he must have known better than
I, that this notion of Rosenmüller, as to Isaiah, caused a controversy in Germany.

for the discrepancy of these statements with that quoted by our Annotator. In the Proem to Isaiah, Part III. Vol. III. Rosenmüller delivers it as his opinion that there are *two grand divisions* of the book of Isaiah, the one containing chapters i.— xxxix. and suiting (with a few exceptions) the time of Isaiah; the other obviously later, as late, indeed, as the close of the Babylonish captivity. *Of this last* he repeatedly speaks *as a separate book*, and it is of *this* that he says (in contrast, I presume, to the other, of which, as I have shewn, he speaks as a whole made up of various parts) in the words quoted by the Annotator, ' that it is the work of a single writer.' What can be said of a person capable of such an artifice? I shall not waste a word upon him.

The second charge against me is founded on another statement in the same page. I have said there that Rosenmüller takes the history of Jonah to be a repetition of the Mythus of Hercules swallowed by the sea monster, and that it was written by a contemporary of Jeremiah. This, says the Annotator, is ' a false and odious exposition of Rosenmüller's opinion, as any one may convince himself who will refer to the Scholia on the minor prophets, Vol. II. p. 356.' Let Rosenmüller speak for himself then. After mentioning the Mythus I allude to, he adds, 'Hunc igitur Mythum, cum aliis vicinarum gentium superstitionibus ad Judæos quoque, uti credibile est, perlatum, hujus libri scriptor, rationibus Hebraicis accommodatum, exornatum et ampliatum, prouti in rem suam conducere videtur, intexuit narrationi ad redarguendos atque corrigendos Hebræos a se compositæ,' &c. In p. 337, he pronounces the whole incidents in Jonah obviously false and absurd; and in p. 359, gives the opinion I have mentioned as to the age of the book.

If the first charge shows the readiness with which my adversary has recourse to artifice, the second will at least serve to prove that it is not because he has any dislike to the method of direct falsehood. After these specimens of his dispositions, I will fairly own that I could not summon up patience to examine his translation. But I take this occasion of telling my German readers that I will not be answerable for any thing in it, for I have casually detected at least one mistranslation which must be intentional *.

The only thing which the translator says besides worth notice, is the supposition that I could

---

* See the reply to Dr. Bretschneider.

not have derived all my information from my own reading or collection, but that I must have been assisted by some German divine. But as this charge is more formally brought forward by Dr. Bretschneider, I refer the reader to my reply to him, and hasten to bid a last farewell to my translator and his friends.

III. ALLGEMEINE KIRCHENZEITUNG.

I. *Allgemeine Kirchenzeitung* * *for Thursday, Oct.* 12, 1826. *No.* 161, *pp.* 1313—1320; *and Saturday, Oct.* 14, 1826. *No.* 162, *pp.* 1321—1327.

II. *Theologisches Literatur-blatt zur Allgem. Kirchenzeitung, for Friday, Dec.* 15, 1826. *No.* 100. *p.* 1809, *and following.*

THE articles here adduced may be safely recommended as specimens of the Rationalist style described by Dr. Staüdlin. It has not often been my lot to meet with any thing so vulgar and so violent; yet, when I consider the writer's object, I ought to feel highly gratified. By far the larger portion

* This journal is published at Darmstadt and conducted by a Dr. Zimmerman. It is considered as one of the regular organs of the Rationalist party; and its influence is undoubtedly very great. I cannot but wonder that the good taste and feeling of Germany have not long ago revolted at it. Never has it been my ill-fortune to see a religious journal in this country, belonging to any class or sect, conducted with such vulgar virulence as this accredited journal of the Rationalists. The temper too displayed in it is dreadful. My reviewer complains of me for wishing for a controul over opinions. Had he not better correct the desire for bodily pains and penalties exhibited in his journal? See the intolerant spirit of persecution displayed (on the strange business in Hanover) in this journal for October 24, 1826. No. 168, pp. 1370, 1371.

of the two first articles is consumed in a most virulent attack on the Church of England, *avowedly* with the intention of consoling those Germans who may have been affected by the statements I have made as to their Protestant Churches, and of proving to them that the Church of England is in the most deplorable state *, notwithstanding the benefit which it enjoys, as I have argued, from the controul exercised over opinion by its Articles and Liturgy. Now in producing these allegations as a set off against my representation of the state of Protestantism in Germany, the writer certainly admits that representation to be generally true.

If I wished effectually to prejudice my readers against him, I should quote his long tirade against our Church; but when I find a person so entirely the dupe of accounts founded either on utter ignorance, or wilful falsehood; when I find him, for

* This is the reply made to me, not only by this writer, but by the translator of my Sermons, both in the Preface, and in a furious note, (p. 14.) in which he accuses the English Church of bigotry, pride, hypocrisy, &c. &c. by Drs. Ammon, Bretschneider, &c. &c. It is singular too that Dr. Ammon, in replying to Dr. Hohenegger, a Catholic Priest, who has produced exactly the same charges as I have against the Rationalists, has no better argument than ' Tu quoque.' See Unveränderliche Einheit, &c. Pt. I. p. 27—29.

example, asserting that the dignitaries of our ca-thedrals are frequently captains in the navy, grooms of the king's bed-chamber, or actors; that many of our bishops are suspected of infidelity; that the salaries of curates are 10*l*. or 12*l*. per annum, and that the Episcopal population is daily sinking into the most frightful depravity *, I consider him as worthy rather of pity than of anger †. At all events, a writer who can be guilty

* The journalist says, he states this on the authority of Dr. Steinkopff. I therefore took the liberty of writing to Dr. Stein-kopff, to mention the use made of his name. His answer states, that he is ' surprised and grieved to learn, that without any know-ledge or sanction of his, his name should have been introduced in a controversy to which he was previously a stranger, and in which he desires to take no part on either side, for he cannot approve of any general and indiscriminate, much less of severe and rash assertions,—whether they may be directed against the national Church of England or against the Protestant Churches of Ger-many (a courteous hint to me)—that he has had the happiness of knowing many truly excellent clergymen, and members of the national Church, and that they know him too well to suspect him of casting unjust reflections on a Church for which he has both felt and manifested the sincerest regard and attachment.' I trust that Dr. Steinkopff will allow that the statements ascribed to him are indeed *unjust* reflections on the Church of England. However this may be, it is pretty clear that the writer of the German article derives all his information from German tra-vellers and residents in England unfavourably disposed to the national Church, and from English dissenters.

† I could heartily wish that on another point the writer spoke

of such errors is not worth the trouble of refutation. And he who in a serious essay can bring
forward, what he calls the ' fat epicurean appearance of the English clergy' as an argument, puts
himself out of the pale of gentlemanly controversy.
In good truth, if his facts were all correct, I cannot
see what inference he would draw from them. If
it is alleged, that something little removed from
Deism has been taught in the German Protestant
Churches, and that the absence of all church authority has enabled the clergy to indulge in these
opinions; what answer is it to say that, in another
church, which in some degree exercises this authority, the clergy are ignorant, and the people
vicious? Is it meant to argue that orthodox clergy

with as little reason as of the infidelity of our bishops, and our
chapters of actors, and navy captains ; but however violent and
vulgar his reproaches are, there is truth in what he says as to
the want of a proper education for the clergy. He states with
great truth the completeness of the courses of divinity in the German universities ; and the abuse of knowledge among a large
party of the German divines can never be alleged as an argument against deeper theological study among ourselves. I do
not mean that to individuals, private study may not answer
as well, or better than public lectures ; but in the Church we
are not to think of individuals, but to form, for the sake of
the Church and the people, a body of learned men—a task certainly very difficult without public instruction of the highest
order.

cannot be learned or conscientious, and that orthodox laymen cannot be moral? or that a good
church is wholly out of the question, and that we
must submit either to licentiousness in opinion,
or to carelessness in practice? If these are not
the inferences from the writer's argument, I am at
a loss to conjecture what they can be. And if
they are, they are assuredly not worth refutation.
I leave him therefore very willingly in possession
of all his strange blunders and his virulence
against the Church of England, and turn to what
he has said especially with regard to me.

I need hardly premise that every decent and
gentleman-like epithet is attached in singular
profusion to my name. The greater part of the
writer's allegations against me are the same as
those of Dr. Bretschneider. Indeed the line of
argument, of blunder, of fallacy, nay of quotations * against me is so entirely the same, that
it is difficult to believe there is not some con-
nexion between them. There is, in both, the
same wilful misunderstanding of all that I have
said as to the controul to be exercised over religious opinions in every Church. Both refer to the
words of my citation from Calixtus as if they were

* As from Reinhard Moral. Part II. p. 774.

my own, both charge me with an inquisitorial spirit—with holding principles subversive of those of the Reformation—with thinking nothing worth attention except the Thirty-nine Articles—with believing that the learning of the Germans is an evil—with having gained all my information from German friends, &c. &c. To these accusations no other reply is necessary than that which will be found under the same heads in the answer to Dr. Bretschneider. The following observations comprise all that is peculiar to this writer.

He charges me with having omitted all notice of the ' sacred names of Morus, Knapp, Keil, Jerusalem, Niemeyer, Rohr, Schuderoff, &c.' That in the list of orthodox writers the name of Knapp should have been noticed is true, and I can only express my regret at the omission and the surprise I felt when I discovered it. It was an omission wholly of mistake, and arose from no want of sincere respect for the name and character of Knapp. Keil and Niemeyer *are* noticed— Rohr's ' sacred name' was omitted, but his principal work, (the Letters on Rationalism, published anonymously) is noticed constantly, so that this accusation is a mere trick. The Journalist may be assured, that in the second edition, Rohr's ' sacred name' shall receive the honour due to it.

Of the others I did not speak, because I had no occasion to notice them. I did not undertake to give a history of every German Divine, but to show the opinions publicly taught in the German churches, and to illustrate my statements by references to various writers.

What follows is an abridgment of all the material parts of the remainder of the articles in question, omitting the scurrility. In commenting on my statement, that the confessions of faith of the Lutheran Church are so long as not to be well adapted for the purpose of subscription, the Journalist asks, whether it is the fault of the modern German Divines that the early Reformers composed inappropriate confessions? and this question is repeated in half-a-dozen forms. The next thing which is at all addressed to me is an invitation to Germany, where I am desired ' not to live with saints, but with Rationalists, and to attend the examinations of some candidates for orders. Then I shall see what a quantity of learning is required of a young man going into the Church. I shall find that he is examined by the *Bible,* and required to adhere to that as his rule of faith. To be sure he may perhaps have a few notions not to be found in Hollaz or Beyer, and may make old gentlemen shake their heads at some of his fancies, but an enlightened college (of examiners) is not anxious on that account. They had rather have thinking young men, capable and desirous of learning, than stiff memory-men, who know forms and definitions, and can jabber their prayers, (this, gentle reader, is intended as a severe blow for the poor English,) and do their business like puppets, but know nothing of real wisdom. Our professors wish for no followers to learn articles of faith by heart, but build up men who enquire, &c. We (Germans) do not stick by what we know, but new necessities present themselves to us. These enquiries have led us to what Mr. Rose calls Atheism *, &c.; but let him not think our state so pitiable. We still make Scripture the ground of our belief. But then its languages must be studied, and all this gives occasion to difference of opinion amongst us, as it did among the old Reformers. Many parts of Scripture, to be sure, have been attacked, but then they have been defended, and not one has yet been *struck out*. We do not deny that we may err, but in a free church the errors of even great men do no mischief. Much amongst us has already become better—our jubilee, in 1817, shewed the warm interest of our

* It is a mere falsehood to say that I brought any such accusation against the Rationalists.

contemporaries in Christianity!—our churches are full when there is a distinguished preacher!! (delightful and improving state,) and very many books of edification and piety are sold. Even Ammon allows that things are improving. Besides, men have too often contended about the words of man, and not of God. Christianity is simple in faith. There is one God and father of all—Jesus Christ, the Son of God, is, *in a peculiar sense,* the Saviour of all, the Spirit of God is our assistance to our sanctification. But what have men made of these doctrines? Does the word Trinity occur in the Bible (delightful argument), or Θεανθρωπος, or satisfaction, &c.? Is it unchristian not to bind one's self to these, or will God condemn men for not agreeing with Athanasius, Calvin, or the Lutheran Churches? Men from all parts of Germany, with very different views, theological and philosophical, agree in *what is necessary and wholesome for all. All keep to the words of the Bible, though they often explain them differently.* It is one Lord whom they own, one Spirit who animates them, though the letter of the Bible is differently worked on; one goes more to sacred history, another to doctrines, but all seek health in Jesus, all are united in heart and love for Christianity.'

A very few words will comprise all the remarks

I have to make on these arguments, and all the reply which I wish to give to the charges of bigotry with which they are plentifully interspersed.

First, then, I do *not* blame modern German Divines for the bad judgment which dictated their confessions of faith—but I blame them because although they *profess* to belong to a Lutheran or a Calvinistic Church, they hold few or none of the points of belief recognized by those Churches, and because they are thus guilty of gross deceit. To accuse me of bigotry for objecting to this is absurd; if the reviewer had read the Sermons he attacks, he would have found me saying, that they who could not agree in the faith of a given Church, should not *enter it,* but *should become openly teachers of Christianity under such a shape as they do admit.* Freedom, I agree with the reviewer, is an excellent thing, but honesty is a still better. And I ask, what sort of honesty is it to enter into a church whose faith you despise, and are perhaps labouring to overthrow? On this subject, however, I have spoken so fully in the reply to Dr. Bretschneider that I deem it unnecessary to add another word. For the same reason I pass over all the absurdities of the journalist with respect to the principles of the Reformation, (principles as much opposed to the practice of

11

the Rationalists as light to darkness,) **and go
on** to what he says on another point, the rule
of faith in the German churches.   They have
still, he says, a guide of faith in the Scripture; an assertion which is directly followed by
a statement, that Scripture is differently interpreted by different persons; and very soon by an
observation, that the words Trinity, Atonement,
God-man, &c. are not found in the Bible, and that
God will never condemn men for disagreeing with
Athanasius, or Augustine.   I am well aware that
the difference between my German adversaries
and myself is here wholly irreconcilable.   It rests
on grounds not visible on the surface.   The simple
fact is, that they have no value for a Church in
our sense of the word, and do not see that any
benefit arises from unity.   Nay, this very journalist argues (p. 1321.) that without reasoning in
a circle, it cannot be proved that the composers
of the symbolical books ever intended to bind
men down to them, or to prevent them from ex-
ercising their free judgment.   That point it is
not my business to argue; but while we disagree
on the foundation, it would of course be vain and
hopeless to discuss the merits or faults of the su-
perstructure.   I address myself to those only who
would admit the advantages of unity in a church,
and to them I distinctly state my conviction, that

for the production of that unity, the assent to Scripture, *not interpreted*, on part of the ministry would be of no avail. But I may spare them and myself the trouble of arguing this point. It has been already admirably done by Balguy *, and I the more willingly refer to him, as the moderation of his opinions is so well known.

My only business with the journalist is to point out the futility of his defence. My accusation against the Rationalists is, that they reject almost all that is positive in Christianity, and consider it only as a moral system under the protection of Providence. The journalist in reply, says, that although the words Trinity, God-man, Atonement, &c. are not in Scripture, yet that the Rationalists acknowledge Christ the Son of God to be *in a peculiar sense* the Saviour of the world. I have already noticed in my Sermons the strange way in which the Rationalists retain the phrases of orthodox Christians and attach a different meaning to them. They seem, like the wit, to think that words were invented only to deceive. This practice is most dangerous to others, and most discreditable to themselves. Most dangerous, I say, to others, because a treacherous friend is always worse than

---

* Charge V. in vol. i. p. 453.

an open enemy. The Deist, (says Soame Jenyns, speaking of the English Rationalists) comes like the multitude with swords and staves to take Jesus; the Rationalist, like Judas, betrays him with a kiss. But it is also most discreditable to themselves. They do not hold the opinions commonly called orthodox; why should they use, in expressing their belief, terms which, from their long usage in conveying those opinions, bear a definite and peculiar signification, different from that which the Rationalists choose to attach to them? Is any good or honest purpose answered by this proceeding? Are they ashamed or afraid of expressing, either collectively or individually, their real opinions? or have they no definite opinions at all? For example, the journalist says that Christ is the Son of God, and in a peculiar sense the Saviour of mankind.   Has he formed to himself any idea of the meaning of the phrase, *Son of God,* as expressed in Scripture ? Does he mean by it one who has any part in the Divine nature, or a mere man, favoured and protected by God? Can he not plainly and honestly tell us what his opinion is ? Again, he says, that Christ was the Saviour of the world.   Does he believe that Christ by his death made satisfaction for our sins, or that his doctrine and example are calculated to save men from vice or misery ? Is it not, I again

ask, easy to state the opinion he has conceived?
Is it not easy to be open, honest, and sincere?
The difficulty, I believe, with many, I say not
with all the Rationalists, is to be open and sincere, and yet to retain any appearance of positive Christianity. And what I complain of in the
journalist and my other opponents is simply this.
I have stated briefly, shortly, and nakedly, the
opinions which the Rationalists hold, and which
they express in their books. When thus stated,
they certainly are not very like Christianity, but
that is not my fault. If they wished to act fairly,
they should correct me, if I have explained their
opinions erroneously; but they should openly
and frankly avow their belief where it is rightly
stated. This is all I could require. I had no intention of entering into controversy with them. I
did not dispute their opinions. I only *stated* them.
It is therefore absurd and unreasonable in a reply to
me, partly to defend their proceedings, and partly
to hold back their real belief. If Wegscheider, or
Bretschneider, or this journalist will simply and
plainly state his opinions, these opinions, though
doubtless differing from one another, would amply
confirm my statements. But were my adversaries
worth complaining of, I might certainly complain
of their want of frankness, and of their endeavour-
ing to destroy the credit of my statements by their

strange mystification, and by their using words in one sense to which they know that another will be attached.   The unwary reader may well be induced to believe that I have traduced the Rationalists, when I state that they believe Jesus to be a mere man, while their champion thus declares that they believe him to be the Son of God and Saviour of the world.   They only who know the Rationalists and their works, know that the two statements are *precisely* the *same*.   It may be well, while speaking on this subject, to notice the admission made by the journalist on these points. If I attended, he says, an examination for orders, I should find perhaps that the candidates did not agree with Hollaz and Beyer, (the old and orthodox expositors of the principles of their Church,) and that an old gentleman might shake his head at them in fear lest religion might suffer.   This is in fact an admission of my statements.   The young Lutheran and Calvinistic ministers are *not* required to hold to the principles of their Churches. It may satisfy the journalist and his friends to say, that the composers of the symbolical books never intended to bind men down to a belief in their exposition of the doctrines of Scripture.   I am not concerned in that question.   I only state two facts, the one, that the German Protestant clergy are allowed to teach what each considers as a true view of Scripture; the other, that in the Churches where this licence is granted, greater or less tendencies to a rejection of all that is positive in Christianity may be very generally discerned.

In conclusion I would beg to observe, that in addition to his scurrility, the journalist does not hesitate to make use of most unfair artifices. The citations which I make from others, he ascribes, whenever he finds it convenient, to me, as the expression of my own opinions. For example, I have quoted a defence offered by some writers for not adhering to the confession of Augsburg, viz. that it was intended only to convey objections against certain errors *. This he chooses to cite as my opinion, and then charges me with inconsistency, for still thinking that subscription to that confession should be required.

Again †, I have quoted Calixtus. His words are charged on me both by Dr. Bretschneider and the journalist as my own, and commented on accordingly.

Such a style of controversy can excite but one

* See p. 116.   † In p. 35, of the Sermons.

feeling. In taking leave of this journalist, indeed,
I can assure him with great truth, that I have
felt only contempt for his scurrility, and regret
that any one who enters on controversy on such
a subject, should so entirely degrade himself as to
shew an utter want of that frankness which be-
comes every honest man, and of the courtesy
which distinguishes a gentleman.

IV. DR. BRETSCHNEIDER.

⸻

CONTROVERSY, although perhaps always in a greater or less degree pernicious, morally speaking, to those who are engaged in it, possesses nevertheless a high degree of interest where *opinions* of importance are at stake; but where its only object is the defence of statements of matters of fact, it appears to me to be of all wearisome things, the most wearisome. To defend them, too, not against open contradiction, not against fair denial, but against special pleading, against verbal criticism, against mistake, perversion, and mistranslation, is a waste of time to which I would never submit for mere personal considerations. Any one who is conscious, however humble his talents or his knowledge may be, that he has been anxious to find out the truth, and careful to state it, may well leave his labours to their fate. In the end justice will be done to his honesty, and the errors, quas aut incuria fudit, aut humana parum cavit natura, will be attributed to their right source, by the only judges about whose verdict he can be solicitous.

The disinclination to undertake any defence of what I have said arising from these feelings, would certainly not be altered by the contents of Dr. Bretschneider's pamphlet *, to which, in the prosecution of my wearisome task, I am now come. I should not, perhaps, speak correctly if I said that it was unworthy even of the bad cause it undertakes to support, but I should be guilty of great injustice to the author, if I did not say that it is quite unworthy of him. I do not feel myself at liberty, however, to pass it over in silence, because, in the present case, the question is *not* a personal one. I have stated that, in the German Protestant Churches, there is nothing to restrain the ministers from pursuing, or from teaching, their own fancies as Christian doctrine; and that a very wide departure from what is ordinarily reckoned Christianity, has taken place in them. Others as well as myself have traced that departure to the absence of all controul over

---

* This pamphlet has been recently translated by the Rev. W. A. Evanson, to whom I beg to offer my best acknowledgments for the handsome manner in which he has spoken of me. I trust that his translation will be generally read by those who have any interest in the question. The weakness and palpable sophistry displayed in it on the one hand, and the irritation and want of common decency on the other, are the strongest arguments I could desire in favour of my statements.

opinion, and have hence inferred the necessity of such controul to the well-being of a Church. If it be true, as Dr. B. would persuade us, that no such departure has taken place, this inference is without foundation. I am therefore anxious to shew, that I have neither misled others, nor have been misled myself on this important subject; and I believe I shall find no difficulty in showing that Dr. B. has not sustained even one of the charges he has brought against me. When I heard of his work, I really flattered myself that I might gain some information from it; and that such casual errors on my part, as a foreigner, undertaking to treat of so wide a subject in so small a space, can hardly escape, would be corrected. I can say, with great truth, that for such correction I should have been most thankful. But I have been miserably disappointed. Instead of the honest and frank reply of a scholar and a gentleman, which I might fairly expect from Dr. Bretschneider, I am constrained to say, that the pamphlet is, from beginning to end, little more than a series of quibbles and evasions. Instead of meeting the question fairly, it catches at careless expressions, dwells on minor points, and quarrels about words.

The method, indeed, which Dr. B. adopts to

procure a verdict against me, can never, I should
imagine, answer his purpose. He commences
with declaring *, that a reply to my statements
would involve a consideration of the history of
the German Churches from the epoch of the Reformation—and that the purpose of such a reply
will be answered if he can destroy my credit, by
convicting me of partiality, ignorance, and incom-
petence. Now such a plan of attack might be
very effectual against an adversary who rested his
statements on his own judgment and his own
knowledge. But the only merit and utility of
my work is this—that it appeals to nothing but
the writings of the Rationalists, and that it does
not profess to rely on any personal observations.
What good then can Dr. B. do to his cause, by
proving me prejudiced and ignorant ? The littera
scripta manet. I may be animated by the worst
spirit, or I may be profoundly ignorant, but the
proof of those propositions will not infuse Christianity into the pages of the Rationalist writers.
I have appealed to volume and page; let Dr. B.
show that the passages I refer to do not appear, or
that they have not the meaning I ascribe to them.
Four or five instances of such proceedings on my
part would indeed establish such dishonesty or in-

* Translation, p. 191.

competence against me, as must close my lips for
ever. Has Dr. B. been able to produce one?

But although I thus demur to my adversary's
choice of ground, I do not refuse to meet him on
it. Before I do so, however, I must show the
reader the spirit in which he comes to the com-
bat. In that part of the contest I willingly allow
him all the superiority he desires. I shall be
compelled, indeed, to speak more harshly than I
wish, but I shall call him no names, and be guilty
of no personalities. Previously to reading his
pamphlet, I felt that respect for him which a reputation for learning always commands; and I
sincerely regret that he has destroyed the sentiment, by showing that he does not possess those
feelings of courtesy and decorum which are at
least the *natural* fruit of literature and learning.
The following specimens will sufficiently show
the temper in which his work is written:

' A true Englishman thinks there can be no
justice, if judges and advocates do not appear in
the courts in stiff coats, gowns, and in the great
wigs of former days, though no one now clothes
himself in so tasteless a manner; and that the constitution will go to wreck if the Lord Chancellor
does not sit on a woolsack. So Mr. Rose thinks

that religion must go to wreck if theology should
throw away the stiff clothing of symbolical doc-
trine-formulas, and if the Liturgy should speak
no longer in the language of the 16th century *.'

Again,

' We should allow Mr. Rose to pay as many
compliments to his colleagues and his superiors
at our cost as he pleases; and should not grudge
him the pleasure of telling his friends, what they
are all persuaded of before, that there is no
country more perfect than England, and no
Church more excellent than the high Episcopal
Church, with its Thirty-nine Articles and its
tedious Liturgy †.'

All this speaks for itself, as do Dr. Bretschneider's courtesies to me,—my bigotry, folly, stu-
pidity, &c. I am not surprised at his want of
temper, because I know the situation of the Rationalists not to be a pleasant one. The hand of
authority is now against them, at least in one
great Protestant country in Germany :— their
violence has produced a reaction—they are split
among themselves—and they see that their ad-

---

* Translation, p. 79.   † Ibid. p. 18.

versaries are gaining strength, and getting into
public favour. All these things make them angry.
They do not like their worst features to be brought
forward. Of some things they have learned to be
actually ashamed—some they would at least disclaim—for some they would apologize—and endeavour, in all ways, to present themselves to
their rulers and their countrymen in as fair a position as possible. Their fears and their jealousies
are indeed indiscribably ridiculous. It would
hardly be believed, that Dr. Bretschneider, thrice
in this short Pamphlet, deprecates the evil which
may result to his party, from my humble work
falling into the hands of German statesmen, ministers, and rulers *! Under these circumstances
I freely forgive Dr. B. his irritability and his want
of courtesy, and proceed to notice his reasonings,
such as they are.

* Translation, pp. 17. 19. 78. I cannot think that Dr. B.
displays any particular wisdom in making these statements. If
German statesmen are likely to listen so readily to my accusations, can they be so utterly destitute of foundation as Dr. B.
would have his reader believe? If a foreigner were to publish
a work, accusing the English Clergy of a leaning to Socinianism,
or to Popery, would they have felt any anxiety as to the impression it was likely to make on the English Government? If my
statements are, indeed, utterly false, Dr. B. pretty openly proclaims the folly or the ignorance of the statesmen to whom he
alludes.

The matter in dispute is this: I have described a very large body of divines in the German Protestant Churches, as having given up all the great doctrines of Christianity; of not considering it as a Revelation in the proper sense of the word, but merely as an excellent moral system, which may be said to come from God, because all that is good comes from him; and of thinking that even that description is to be applied to such parts of Christianity only as recommend themselves to our reason. I have said that these opinions were very general, though not universal, but that they are now beginning to lose their credit. The only point then which can give Dr. Bretschneider as plaintiff, or myself as defendant, any just claim to the reader's attention, is this, are these statements correct, and if they are, are the opinions to which they relate defensible?

But instead of any denial, or any justification of the facts mentioned in the libel of which he complains, Dr. B. brings forward his first charge of prejudice and exaggeration against me *; and the words on which he founds it are some in which I have described Rationalism as ' a dreadful pest,'—' threatening the destruction of all that is dear, sacred, and holy.'

* Translation, p. 20.

I need hardly observe, that an advocate who had any reliance on the strength of his cause, would not, when he accused a whole volume of exaggeration, rest the proof of his charge on a single sentence. If the charge be just, he could not be at a loss for far more ample confirmation of it. However, if he likes to set his cause upon a cast, I have no objection to stand the hazard of the die.

That the words he has quoted were used wholly and entirely in reference to *Christianity,*—that the very page from which they are extracted proves this,—that in no one part of my work is there the smallest intention of accusing the Rationalists of either Atheism or immorality,— nay, that the very sum and substance of my ac- cusation is, that in their doctrines there is a con- stant tendency to Deism, and in many cases a perfect identity with it, every candid reader will admit : every candid reader would, therefore, take these expressions in the sense in which they were clearly and evidently meant, and understand me as asserting, that the Rationalist doctrines threaten with destruction all that is dear, sacred, and holy in Christianity—that in the Rationalist system, in a word, all the hopes which the Chris- tian reposes in Jesus the eternal God, as the Re- deemer of man alike from the power and the

punishment of sin, are reduced to nothing.   But
of such candour—(it would be more fitly called
honesty)—I can rarely accuse Dr. Bretschneider :
he has here and elsewhere descended to an artifice
unworthy of him.   A charge which is preferred
in one sense, and which in that sense is *just*, he
tacitly assumes to be made in another in which it
is *unjust*, which was not intended by me, but of
which the words composing the accusation are by
dint of torture susceptible.   In this second sense
he denies the charge with truth in the *letter*, but
not in the *spirit*, because he evidently expects the
unsuspicious reader to understand the denial as
applying to that sense in which the charge was
made.   In the present case his logic has been
obviously this :—In speaking of *Christianity*, I
say that the Rationalists would destroy all that is
sacred, dear, and holy :—that he cannot and does
not deny ; but he tacitly assumes that this proposition is *not confined* to Christianity, but *general*.
Then he argues that a belief in God and a love
for morality are things dear, sacred, and holy.
But to these the Rationalist opinions threaten no
evil,—therefore, my accusations must arise from
mere prejudice and exaggeration.   By this petty
artifice, Dr. B. has given an apparent denial to
my statement, while in fact he has taken no notice of it, and accuses me of dealing unjustly, by

the use of such strong expressions, with even Bahrdt, whom he seems to consider as the weakest and worst of the writers I have noticed. Secure in the position which I have never attacked, viz. that the Rationalist writers believe in a God, and wish well to morality, his chivalry in defence of even those from whose opinions he dissents, knows no bounds. Although Wegscheider goes far, as he says, beyond him in Rationalism, he is quite willing to defend even him from the charge of wishing to destroy all that is sacred, dear, and holy *, which charge, *in the sense ascribed to it by Dr. B.*, let me repeat, I never made. It would be sufficient to notice this, and pass over Dr. B.'s defence of Wegscheider, with which I have no concern ; but that defence will throw some light on the matter in question, that is to say, the opinions of the Rationalists. And I am anxious, not like Dr. B. to avoid the general question, but to meet it. I shall therefore say a few words with respect to Wegscheider, to whose name I have so often, in my Sermons, referred. I did so for the

---

* Dr. B. asserts that Dr. Ammon and himself now belong to the same party. Yet Dr. Ammon speaks, as my readers will see below, of ' Rationalism, which dries up the heart, and her companion, Unbelief.' Before Dr. B. attacked me, he should have desired his brother in arms, not to use declarations so nearly resembling mine.

E

reason stated in my Preface,—that his work contained a general view or summary of the opinions of his party, and references to their works. His private opinion was a matter of no consequence. The opinion of one man is no criterion of that of a Church, and therefore when I quoted him, I quoted him only because I found, from a comparison of his work with others, that he spoke briefly the sentiments of a large body of persons who agreed with him in opinion. A defence of Wegscheider in particular, was therefore quite a superfluous piece of gallantry on Dr. B.'s part; but as he chooses to make Wegscheider an especial party to the warfare, and wishes to prove, or rather to *appear* to prove me guilty of prejudice, in saying that the opinions held by that writer lead to the destruction of all that is sacred, dear, and holy, I have no objection to shew that the charge, in the sense I intended it, though made against a body, is perfectly applicable to Wegscheider in particular. Dr. B. tells us *, that that divine not only believes in a God, his creation, providence, the free agency of man, the immortality of the soul, and future retribution, and has amply proved these points in his work; but that with respect to the positive institutions of Christianity, he so ex-

---

* Translation, p. 21. 25.

presses himself as to recognize ' whatever articles of faith are necessary for a Christian life.' What sense Dr. B. may choose to attach to these words, which he prints in large letters, as if of great importance, I am not concerned to inquire; but I assert, and will prove, that Wegscheider rejects every thing peculiar to Christianity, which Christians deem, dear, sacred, and holy, with one single exception. Dr. B. produces three passages from Wegscheider to prove his assertion, which would prove any thing else just as well. But let us see what they do prove. Wegscheider, like many Deists, recognises the excellence of the Christian system of morality; and, on the grounds which I just now stated, (viz. that all that is good comes from God,) calls it *divine truth.* On the same grounds he dignifies the Bible, as he might all that is true in Plato or Epictetus, with the name of the Word of God*. The first passage then which Dr. B. quotes †, states, that ' there is no doubt that the canon of the New Testament con-

---

* It is painful and disagreeable to accuse a large body of men of artifice; but such an accusation against the Rationalists is susceptible of the fullest proof. They use the words which orthodox Christians use *in a different sense*, and thus frequently defend themselves by a disgraceful juggle. (See the Reply to the Allgem. Kirchen-Zeitung.) Is not this quite below men of learning and character?

† Translation, p. 22.

tains the most ancient and credible documents of
the Christian religion, and the *divine truth* which
it sanctions.'   In the next *, which follows, as
Dr. B. says, a denial that Jesus and the Evan-
gelists had any immediate inspiration from God,
and an admission of their claim to a mediate one,
Wegscheider expresses his wish that ' all the ar-
tificial conjectures and difficult and useless questions as to Revelation and the inspiration of
Scripture, which have been stirred in a *recent*
age, being laid aside, the origin of Christianity
and Scripture should be derived from God,' (in
the way above explained,) ' and that its contents,
which are truly divine, should be recommended
to men as if proceeding from God, and being his
true word, and thus transferred to the advantage
of daily life.'   Dr. B. says, that in these sentiments every Supernaturalist will join;—and I
add, so will every reasonable Deist.

But still farther, in another passage †, Wegscheider states, that as the author of the Christian
religion united great sanctity and piety to the
purest precepts of virtue, and *thus accommodated
himself most admirably to the divine will*, the help
and favour of Providence assisted him *wonderfully*,

* Translation, p. 22.   † Ibid. p. 24.

and therefore the institution of Christianity is
most justly accounted the work of God; and with
equal justice Jesus and his Apostles are accounted
messengers and ministers of God. A most happy
advocate the Rationalists have, doubtless, in Dr.
Bretschneider. The question is, Do they believe
that Christianity is a Divine Revelation, and do
they receive (among others) the doctrines of the
Divinity of Christ, and the Atonement made for
man's sin by his blood? Dr. Bretschneider does
not even affect to say that they do. But, says
he, one of the most violent of them allows that
Christianity is an excellent moral dispensation,—
that whatever is good comes from God—that
Christianity may therefore be well said to come
from him,—and that the New Testament contains
a credible account of it; nay, that as Jesus was a
most excellent person, God favoured his plan,
and so he and his Apostles may be justly called
messengers of God! Could Wegscheider say less,
without openly professing to oppose Christianity?
Nay, even if he did openly oppose it, could he
deny the excellence of its morality? What his
real opinions are, I will now show; and I will first
state his opinion as to the immortality of the soul.
It is taken, be it remembered, from a book called,
' Institutiones Theologiæ *Christianæ* Dogmaticæ.'
After stating how the doctrine of a future life is
presented in the Old and New Testaments, and

as an ecclesiastical doctrine, he delivers his judgment on it in words, of which the following are
an abridgment :

' To decide on these opinions, we must now
see, under the guidance of sound reason, on what
arguments the doctrine of the immortality of the
soul can be built.

' I. The first is the historical argument, from
the consent of almost all nations and philosophers; but this only shows that human reason
may be easily led to adopt the opinion.

' II. We have philosophical arguments ;

' (1.) Theoretical, viz.

' a. Metaphysical ones, arising from the nature of the soul.

' β. Teleological; deduced partly from the
analogy of nature, in which we see nothing perish,
but rather from death enter on a new life ; and
partly from an accurate consideration of human
nature struggling on perpetually to a greater degree of perfection.

' γ. Theological; arising from true ideas of
God, the just, wise, and benignant Creator of the
universe and of man.

' (2.) Practical; having a reference to man's moral constitution, and especially his consciousness of a moral law, which demands a more perfect unity of virtue and happiness in another life.

' If we examine these arguments, especially the theologic and moral ones, which have not only a probability like the others, but the highest evidence, we shall find that they agree with the purer * and more simple doctrines of Scripture on

* He explains the meaning of this word elsewhere by saying, that there are two opinions on the immortality of the soul propounded in the New Testament. The one of which simply, and avoiding all the figments about Hades, teaches that we are at once to pass to a future life : the other accommodated to Jewish notions, and speaking of a resurrection of the body, and of the good and evil, at the coming of Christ, which was taught to be near at hand (p. 555) ; and he afterwards (p. 571) tells us in so many words, that the resurrection of the body is a notion arising from the imperfect fancies of uncivilized men—that it is so joined with the *mythi* in the New Testament, relating to the Messiah and his return to life, that it can only be explained and defended as they can ; and that though taught in the New Testament, it must be allowed, that either Jesus favoured the opinions of his countrymen, or rather that the Apostles put such a sentiment in his mouth as the Messiah, whose province they wrongly judged of from certain vulgar notions of the Jews and some allegorical and obscure sayings of his own ! If I ever mistake Wegscheider's meaning, I trust, that his barbarous Latin will be my excuse. I can truly say, that I *endeavour* to understand and represent it fairly.

the subject, and teach that this life and the next
are so connected, that the one will instantly suc-
ceed the other; and that the soul, with feeling
and consciousness and a new organ, (as it were a
more subtle body, for finite minds, without limit
of space and a bodily nature, can hardly be conceived,) will survive after the death of the earthly
body.'

What then! The Christian's hope of a future
life rests, as it did before Christ came into the
world, on metaphysical and teleological and moral
proofs! He did not bring immortality to light
by the Gospel! It is not now *more certain* than
before his coming, that there is a house not made
with hands beyond the grave!

Perhaps it would be unnecessary to add any
more. But whatever is not actually brought forward, is always denied by my adversaries. And
I will therefore farther state, that the doctrines of
the Trinity *, the Godhead of Christ, the person-
ality of the Spirit, the justification of sinners by
Christ's death, with all the consequences of that
doctrine,—in one word, every thing positive in
Christianity, except the doctrine of Christ's re-

* Translation, p. 277.

surrection, (to which, strange to say, a sort of assent is reluctantly given, and which Wegscheider considers as a proof of God's satisfaction with Christ's conduct, but not of a divine mission!)—are treated by him as perfect absurdities—the mere dreams of the Apostles, (as in the case of the atonement,) or the fancies of ecclesiastics. Nay, farther still, it is the express doctrine of this writer, in the very section from which Dr. B. takes his second extract, that all which the Apostles taught was only intended for people of their own day, though we may draw from it a knowledge of Christianity, which may be accommodated to *the illumination of a more cultivated age* *.

* The account given by Dr. Staüdlin of Wegscheider may perhaps be more satisfactory to some readers than mine. He tells us then, that it is Wegscheider's opinion, that a supernatural religion is at variance with God's perfect power, wisdom, and goodness,—that all peculiar miracles and mysteries must be explained on natural grounds,—that Christianity was made known to men by a particular divine providence, and deserves to be called divine,—that it comes the nearest to the idea of a true religion,—that still it was shaped so as to meet the particular feelings of the age in which it was promulgated, and mixed with mythi and traditions,—that Jesus or his disciples in *matter* and *form* and *negatively, accommodated* themselves to existing circumstances—that of *positive* accommodation to errors on the part of Jesus, there is no clear proof in the New Testament: but that, if

He who so thinks may talk of a mediate inspiration and may not deny the excellence of Christianity, but he denies every thing that raises it above a human system,—every thing, in short, which gives comfort to man's mind, sensible of

it is admitted, we must assume, that he could not in all points raise himself above the views of his contemporaries, and that there were some things which he knew nothing of,—that Christianity is not only subjectively but objectively perfectible,—that it was first delivered to rough men, and is not perfect. Miracles, in the Biblical sense, are only extraordinary circumstances, calculated to excite belief. In a strict sense they cannot be reconciled with God's perfection,—the more ignorant and superstitious a people is, the more they are inclined to believe in them. The witnesses are not always credible, they tell us their own belief —introduce mythi, &c. The belief in miracles is prejudicial to virtue, and they are not sufficient tests of truth, a declaration on which I need not add that Dr. B. comments at great length. Neither are prophecies ;—these, indeed, if admitted, tend to fatalism. But there are no clear undoubted prophecies in the Bible. Some were never fulfilled ; some were spoken (or at least pointed out) *after* the events. Jesus *accommodated* several to himself,—his disciples raised the idea of him too high,—he appears only as a man, when the history of him is stripped of its mythic and poetic ornaments. There are doctrines in the New Testament quite at variance with those which teach the atonement. He did not rise from the dead; for he did not die on the cross. In the promise of a general resurrection, he either spoke according to Jewish notions, or his disciples ascribe to him their own notion of the Messiah. Staüdlin's History of Supernaturalism and Rationalism, p. 302—307.

human weakness, and suffering under the sense of it,—every thing which Christians deem ' sacred, dear, and holy.' Have I, in using those words, (and speaking as a Christian,) said too much? Have I any reason to fear the verdict of Christians on this point? But even if it were true that I had used stronger language than I ought, does that alter the case? Is it not still true that Wegscheider and numberless other Rationalists deny what Christians deem the most essential of Christian doctrines? What matters it, then, whether I have spoken properly or improperly? What would it avail the criminal on his trial, if, instead of answering the charge, he complained that the witness judged too harshly of its heinousness? And what can it avail the Rationalist to say that I am prejudiced or weak, if the charge I bring is true? The *fatalis arundo* will stick in the side it has pierced, though it may have been aimed by an unskilful or a treacherous hand. And the Rationalists should remember, that the question concerns not me, but them.

This defence of Wegscheider is the single argument on which Dr. B. rests the charge of prejudice and party spirit which he has brought against me. It is not calculated, I think, to give one very high ideas of his powers as a controver-

sialist, and the remarks with which he concludes
it do not entitle him to a very exalted rank as a
logician.   After all, he argues *, What is the
mighty difference between the opinions of Messrs.
Wegscheider and Rose ? One husbandman thinks
that the sun and rain which ripen his corn, are
sent by the immediate volitions of the Deity,
while the other attributes these blessings to the
general but benignant laws of his Providence. It
would be unjust to reckon one of these men to
possess a proper sense of religion, and the other
to be deficient in it.   Yet there is no other difference of opinion between Messrs. Wegscheider
and Rose, as to the origin of Christianity ; the
one holds that Jesus was supernaturally enlightened, while the other attributes his knowledge of
divine truth to the ordinary or mediate working
of Providence!   After this specimen of Dr. B.'s
logic, my readers may judge with what peculiar
justice he complains of bad reasoning in others.
Does he really see no difference between the
matter in dispute and his illustration of it ? Does
he really fail to perceive that in his illustration, *the
facts of the case* are *confessedly* in the ordinary
course of nature, while in the matter illustrated—
(I beg pardon for the word)—the first point to

* Translation, p. 25.

settle is, whether they are so or not ? Before his analogy will hold, he must *prove*, what he tacitly assumes, that the miracles are no miracles ; and when he has done that, I shall be happy to argue this part of the subject with him.

Having dispatched the charge of *partiality*, Dr. Bretschneider next comes * to the head of *ignorance* and *confined views;* and two pages and a half are devoted to accusing me of believing that nothing is right except the thirty-nine articles, and of never having subjected my belief to any examination, nay, of thinking that religious belief ought not to be subjected to any. This latter charge, which is made by the writer in the Allgemeine Kirchenzeitung, rests on my having said that a minister of the Church ' must not think his own thoughts, but teach what the Church teaches.' The change is rung on these words till one is quite weary. Whether these writers misunderstand them wilfully or not, I know not ; although their meaning is so plain, from the context, that I can hardly acquit them of wilful perversion. The case in a few words is this. The Rationalists do not think it dishonest to become ministers of a Church holding definite

* Translation, pp. 26, 27.

opinions, and to disbelieve and deny all its doctrines. I do. While I am a minister of a given Church, holding given doctrines, I cannot in common honesty consider myself at liberty to teach any others. If I do, I violate my trust. But, say they, What will you do, if you come to *disbelieve* those doctrines? Surely there can be little difficulty in finding an answer to that question. I must either renounce the situation I hold, as I cannot discharge the conditions on which it was given to me, or I must renounce all pretensions to the character of an honest man. It is a most false and unjust charge to say, that I wish to suppress inquiry into the evidences or the doctrines of Christianity. I have too deep a conviction of its truth, not to desire that full activity should prevail in every department of theological research. I do not indeed desire that men should begin with *assuming* the falsehood of much which is taught in the Church to which they belong, and then exert all their ingenuity in getting rid of it. Let their inquiries be candid, and then let them be as wide as possible. If any one is led by those researches to disbelieve the doctrines of his Church, let him cease to be a minister of it, and not go on, like the Rationalists, to live under its shelter and deride its doctrines. If he will not voluntarily act like an honest man, let him be compelled to do so.

But, argues Dr. B.*, Mr. Rose confesses the great pre-eminence of the Germans in other branches of study, and yet he is foolish enough to expect that in theology they should stand still. Nay, he ascribes all their errors to their carrying their inquiries *too far*, as if any research could be too deep, &c. &c. 'What an idea,' says he, ' must Mr. Rose have of literary research, if he thinks there can be such a thing as a " *too deep consideration*," a " *too deep* exploring in philosophical grounds," a point at which men ought to rest in *superficial* causes.' The passage on which Dr. B. founds his last assertion is as follows in the original. The errors of most of the Germans ' are owing to the perplexity arising from too deep consideration, from an unwillingness to rest on *obvious* causes,' &c. The Translator of my Sermons has most dishonestly rendered the word † *obvious* by *oberflächlichen*, which signifies *superficial;* and has thus made me say, that the Germans are unwilling ' to rest on superficial causes.' I say *dishonestly,* because the word *su-*

* Translation, pp. 29, 30, 31.

† Mr. Evanson, in an anxious desire to do me justice, has given my real words in his translation, and not those which are put into my mouth by my translator. Dr. B.'s argument, therefore, does not tell so well for himself in the translation as in the original.

perficial really occurs *only* four lines lower, and
is rendered also by *oberflächlichen;* and I say *dis-*
honestly, because I have already convicted this
Translator of shameless dishonesty. Whether Dr.
B. reads English or not, I cannot decide. He does
not always quote the exact words of the translation; but still I am unwilling to consider him in
the same light as my dishonest Translator. Yet
he too, who has of course taken advantage, page
after page, of my (apparently) saying, that the
Germans are unwilling to rest in *superficial*
causes, has * taken *unfair* advantage of another
expression in the same passage. I may perhaps
allow that the phrase *too deep consideration*
might be altered, so as to express my obvious
meaning better; but Dr. B. could not fail to see
why it was used. A Quarterly Reviewer had remarked, that Niebuhr had *not considered* certain
points; and in reply to his remark I said, ' German errors do not arise in general from *want of*
consideration, but from *too deep consideration,* and
from not resting on *obvious* causes.' Whether
that account of the Germans is *true,* I leave to
others to judge; but it is at least *intelligible,* and
it describes a state of mind not only intelligible,
but constantly found in individuals. Enough

---

* Translation, p. 31.

however of this.   Let Dr. B. enjoy all the advantage he can from mistranslation of my words and perversion of my meaning ; this will not alter the case, nor does it serve as a defence of his opinions. —I go on to observe that his statement, as to the necessary influence of progress in *other* sciences on the state of theology, involves the whole matter in dispute.   No one can doubt that progress in learning and real knowledge will throw light on many dark places in theological study; but the question is still as it was, Does Christianity come *directly* from God; and if it does, are we to expect progress in that as in other things ? Has God taught us what we are to believe, or are we to go on finding this out ourselves ? If we are, Christianity is of course not a revelation.   Now this is the view of many of the Rationalists, who will not allow the existence of a revelation, and so treat Christianity like a human science. When they have *proved* that this view is just, no objection can be offered to their proceedings,—but let them do that first.   But, says my antagonist*, Mr. Rose really wishes to put a forcible stop to this progress of theology, and speaks of the absolute necessity of some check and restraint over the human mind in every religious society, and espe-

---

* Translation, p. 31.

F

cially over its ministers. Then follow three
pages of the inquisition, and Galileo *, and civil
punishments, and the use of actual force †, in
checking free enquiry, and the certainty that neither the Reformation nor Christianity itself could
ever have existed if my principles had been acted
on.   Let me console Dr. B. by assuring him, that
by *check and restraint* I mean neither whips, nor
racks, the fire, the sword, nor the dungeon ; but
simply, as I have stated elsewhere in the Sermons,
and as he knows I have stated, *this one check,* that
the Church should be able to say to those who
disbelieve her doctrines, what they ought to say
to themselves, ' Quit the ministry of a Church,
the doctrines of which you hold to be false ; be
honest to the Church, to the people, and to your-
self.'   Such restraint, I take it, would not have
operated unfavourably towards the Reformation,
nor to any other *honest* cause.

* It is curious that one of the organs of Liberalism in this
country (the London Magazine) has proved very clearly this
year, what most persons knew before, that Galileo was not *per-
secuted* at all.   But what could induce a *Liberal* Journal to take
the side of such odious animals as Priests, even if they happen
to be in the right? The wonder may perhaps be diminished,
when we remember that the persons defended are not Protestant,
but Popish Priests, who at present are in an unnatural coalition
with the Liberals.

† Translation, p. 33.

Dr. B. then * triumphs over me in three pages more, for what he considers as a most extraordinary contradiction in two of my statements. In one place I have remarked, that perhaps I should hardly have deemed it wise to bring forward such a mass of mischievous and evil opinions, had not a great part of them already been spread abroad in this country by Rosenmüller and Kühnöl. Just below I have said, that I have not felt it necessary to offer any thing in *refutation* of the Rationalist opinions, for that in nine instances out of ten their opinions have been expressed a thousand times in Deistical writers, and as often refuted.

Supposing this to be a contradiction, let me ask once more, What good does Dr. B. get to his cause by proving it so? There are distinct charges made against his friends for their opinions, and the very pages of the work which contain those opinions are given. He should either prove that the citations are wrong, or that the opinions are right. To prove that I have written carelessly can do him and them no possible good. But in good truth, is there either carelessness or contradiction in what I have said? In the *very*

* Translation, pp. 33—36.

next sentence to that which he has quoted, the solution of this mighty enigma is given, as it has
been half a dozen times before in the work.
‘ The novelty of the Rationalists’ opinions is the
fact of their being now expressed by persons
calling themselves believers, and holding high
situations in a Christian Church.’   This is what I
meant—simply, that is to say, that I might perhaps have hardly deemed it wise to bring forward
as the opinions of men, in profession pious *Christians*, and holding high stations as Christian
Teachers in Universities and Churches, positions
fit only for infidels, but well adapted to be hailed
with rapture by a *low* and *liberal* age.   This is in
fact so obvious, that nothing but prejudice could
have perverted it.

Dr. B. in this part of his argument *, asks,
though rather out of place, what possible good
the restraint over opinion in our Church, of which
I boast, has done ? Is it not the fact, says he, that
the Church of England is diminishing constantly,
while Unitarian, Methodist, Quaker, and Inde-
pendent communities daily increase ? I *might*
answer, that it is *not* the fact that the Church is
now losing its numbers ;—but supposing it were,
I should still have an answer to Dr. B.'s question.

* Translation, p. 36.

Doubtless it is true that *separation* from the
Church has taken place. Now such separation
certainly could not happen in Germany: how
should it? From what is a man to separate there?
He may hear in the German Protestant Churches,
even according to Dr. Bretschneider's own confessions, pure Naturalism, a sort of belief in Christianity, Socinianism, here and there orthodox
doctrines, and even Mysticism. *I* teach Rationalist doctrines; my next neighbour preaches Supernaturalist opinions. He who does not like
one, may easily go to the other, without quitting
the Church. Indeed in quitting the Church what
would he quit? Could he say, or could any one
tell him? Why should a man give up, as not suiting him, what has been and may be put in any
shape he pleases? With us, on the contrary, the
Church teaches definite opinions, be they right or
wrong. Dr. Wegscheider could not in the English
Church laugh at revelation; nor could Dr. Bretschneider ask in an English pulpit, who can find
the words Trinity or Atonement in the New Testament? This then is the effect of the control
over opinions in the Church of England. Countless thousands of Christians, who believe (right
or wrong is not the question) certain doctrines,
and consider them as pure and genuine Christianity, know that in the Church they shall hear

those doctrines, and not be subject, as they would
be in Germany, either to hear a variety of Christian, semi-Christian and demi-semi-Christian doctrines, or to hear no Christian doctrine at all; to
hear practical theology reduced to mere expediency, on which certainly no difference of opinion
can take place, and so to lose every thing which
consoles and cheers the mortal, the frail and the
penitent.   This, I say, is the good which the
control in the Church of England has done.

But next *, Dr. B. decides that I am incapable
of writing on the subject I have undertaken, because it is clear I do not know the difference between *religion* and *theology*, as I have spoken of
the ' Protestant Religion in Germany,' when I
should have said ' Protestant Theology.'   I am
not, I fear, as nice as I ought to be in the choice
of words; but with due deference to Dr. B. I
shall still beg to use such words as express my
meaning, even though he should not understand
them.   I did *not* mean the *Theology* when I said
the *Religion.*   I meant to give an account of the
state of Protestantism altogether, of the Church,
the Theology, &c. &c. of the Protestants.   And
whether the word *Religion* is the best which
could be chosen, I know not; but it is commonly

* Translation, p. 37.

used in the sense I have assigned to it. The next attack * is on my ignorance of the relation of Reason and Revelation, and on my complaints that nothing is recognized which the Rationalists do not consider as agreeable with reason. Mr. Rose, says Dr. B., must allow that a man must examine to know whether Christianity is true, as he cannot know previous to examination which of the positive religions in the world he ought to respect †. This is assuredly true, and I have said so ; but Dr. B.'s complaint is, that I wish the examination to apply to the external and not the internal nature of the religion. This is true *only in part.* ' Must I not,' says Dr. B. ' if any thing is offered to me as coming from God, inquire if it is worthy of him ? Would Mr. Rose receive the doctrine that God does not govern the world, but exists in eternal inactivity, even if supported by any number of miracles ?'- What is to be said of such a reasoner,—what answer to be given him ? He states what he thinks and what he knows his antagonist will think, a palpable false-hood, and then asks, whether it could be believed even if attested by a host of miracles ? Dr. B. must have strange ideas of miracles, and of the

* Translation, pp. 37, 38.

† This charge is made also by the writer in the Allgemeine Kirchenzeitung.

omnipotence of God. I presume that there is nothing very singular in my opinion that miracles * are proofs, if they exist, of the truth of Christianity, and that therefore it is first of all advisable to ascertain whether there are any miraculous manifestations of divine power in favour of Christianity. The Rationalists reason differently. They desire us first to examine the doctrines of Christianity, and see whether they are such as recommend themselves to reason : if not, to reject them at once, or keep only such as do so: and as to the miracles, as they would be of no use at all events, the moderate Rationalists take little or no account of them, and the others exert all their learning and talents to explain them away. Dr. Bretschneider † says indeed, in the regular phrase of the Socinian, that the Rationalists reject nothing but what is *contrary* to reason, not what is *beyond* it, and asserts that that principle is recognized by many writers among them. Words are easily used, but I appeal to their practice, and am quite contented to take the decision of any one at all acquainted with their works.

* On the comparative value of the miracles and doctrines of Christianity, see what I have said below in the reply to Dr. Ammon.

† Translation, p. 39.

But Dr. B. thinks * that I confound reason with self-will, (the mistake, let him be assured, is not on *my* side,) and complains bitterly of my saying, that the German Churches ' boast of it as their very highest privilege, and the very essence of a Protestant Church, that its opinions should constantly change ;' and of my citing, in proof of this position, the words of Schröckh, who says that ' our divines recognize the necessity of inquiring, correcting, and ameliorating their belief as often as any new views require it, and do not deny the possibility of making that belief more free from false explanations and arbitrary adjuncts firmer in some parts, and more connected in all.' Dr. B. with that want of candour which characterises his pamphlet, *omits all notice* of the only part of this sentence, which is of any real consequence, viz. *the first*, which states, that the Protestant ' Divines recognize the necessity of correcting and ameliorating their belief as often as any new views require it ;' and asks, very triumphantly, in allusion to the latter clause, whether freeing our faith from arbitrary adjuncts and false explanations is an abdicating of faith itself? It is not necessary to do any thing more than point out this gross instance of disingenuousness.

* Translation, p. 40.

Dr. B. goes on to argue, that I have entirely perverted Schröckh's meaning; for he is not speaking of Religion or Christianity itself, nor of the divine contents of the Bible, but of the theological system of the Church. And Church doctrines, he says, are in all Churches only a public exposition on the part of a certain number of Christians, how they understand the Biblical doctrines, and what they hold to be such. This I confess, is beyond me, if intended as a proof that I have quoted unfairly, or misunderstood Schröckh. I certainly understood that by the word *belief*, he meant the view of the Biblical doctrines entertained and professed by the divines of whom he spoke, and I have quoted his words under that impression; but if Dr. B. prefers his own exposition, let us take it by all means. ' The German divines then,' according to that exposition, ' recognize the necessity of inquiring, correcting, and ameliorating their *view of Biblical doctrines* as often as any new notions require it.' This is exactly what I accused them of doing. To-day they may believe in the Trinity, to-morrow they may be Arians, the third day Socinians, in each case professing to rely on the Bible. Is this desirable or not? Can this be right or not? But farther, says Dr. B. this is no new matter, for the Reformers claimed the same right, and expressly

11

said, that they looked on symbolical writings only as historical testimonies how the teachers of the Church at particular times understood and explained Scripture. And to prove this, he gives * a very long quotation from the Formula Concordiæ, saying,—what does the reader think ?—'that Creeds, &c. have not the *auctoritas judicis* which is due to Scripture alone, but only give a testimony for our religion, and explain it, and show how at each period the Scripture, in controverted points, was understood and explained by the then Doctors of the Church!!' In good truth, Dr. Bretschneider is a marvellous logician! This, he maintains, is a claim on the part of the Reformers to exactly the same right as Schröckh claims for modern divines, viz. that of inquiring into the theological system of the Church. The Reformers say, for example, ' the Nicene Creed recognizes the Divinity of our Lord. We do not believe this point of faith on the authority of the Nicene Creed, but on that of Scripture ; but we appeal to the Nicene Creed to show that its authors understood Scripture as we do.' And this, it seems, means that it is very right and reasonable to adopt Luther's Catechism to-day, and the Racovian to-morrow! I confess I am unable to com-

---

* Translation, p. 42.

prehend this ratiocination; nor can I think that what follows does any great credit to my critic's understanding. ' Mr. Rose,' says he *, ' confounds Church systems of doctrine and Biblical doctrines, which are very different things. Let Mr. Rose shew us a single place in the Old or New Testament where the words Trinity †, Persons in the Godhead, Atonement, Predestination, Original Sin, &c. or a single place where it is said, the Son is the second person in the Trinity, the Spirit the third, the Father the first, &c. or, the Son has atoned for sins, or, Man has through Adam's fall lost the use of his reason and free-will. All these things are only the Church system on particular expressions of Scripture, and explanations how the Church expounds the Bible, and what consequences it draws from certain expressions.' Be it so. And what does Dr. B.'s logic prove? Simply

---

* Translation, p. 44.

† If the German Rationalists supply the English Socinians with a little learning, the Unitarians, it seems, repay them with a few arguments in defence of their common views. This argument is a favourite piece of folly on the part of the Unitarians. I remember a cobbler of that persuasion at Brighton, sticking up a placard in his window, offering a reward to any one who would find the word Trinity in the Bible. This argument is repeated at great length, and almost in Dr. B.'s words, in the Allgemeine Kirchenzeitung.

that certain technical expressions, used for convenience sake, are not found in the Bible, and that doctrines, some of which are, in the opinion of countless thousands, to be found in every page of the New Testament, are not put there in a certain form, approved by Dr. Bretschneider! His confusion, indeed, on the matter of *belief* in points of faith is beyond description. He thinks that, if a technical word is used to describe certain assertions supposed to be in Scripture, and if he can show that the technical word is not used in Scripture, the doctrine which it represents cannot be there; and that if I sum up the scattered statements of Scripture in two or three clear but formal propositions, these propositions are mere Church doctrines. Of course I may or may not be right in my view of the doctrine of Scripture; but to prove me wrong it is not sufficient to show that my technical word or my proposition is not in Scripture, but that they are *erroneous* substitutes for what is *.

* Dr. B. has been guilty of another piece of disingenuousness here. In quoting the opinion of Reinhard on subscription to articles, he calls him, very rightly, a strict *Supernaturalist*, having previously in p. 39 classed him with ' our theologians Ammon, Döderlein,' &c. *men with whom he disagreed entirely.* This is done doubtless to throw dust in the eyes of those who know Reinhard's character. If ' our theologians' Ammon and Döderlein

However, Dr. B. * soon leaves this part of the subject, to show that I do not understand the origin of the English Church, because I say that our Reformers did not pretend to discover new views, but to return to the old ones held by the

are like Reinhard, a strict Supernaturalist, how unjust must accusations like Mr. Rose's be! But I have a single word to say on the quotation from Reinhard. That writer says, that by subscription to articles, a man does not bind himself unconditionally to maintain as unalterable the opinions which at the time of subscription he thinks true,—that he is bound to enquire unceasingly,—and that every one must declare for himself whether the tenets of a particular Church agree with Scripture, which is the ultimate appeal. This passage Dr. B. brings to show how foolish I am in requiring more than so strict a Supernaturalist as Reinhard. But here Dr. B. as usual, either wilfully or ignorantly, misunderstands my meaning. I do not complain of the Rationalists for *enquiring*, if their enquiries are fair and candid, but for their line of conduct *after enquiring*. I agree entirely with the spirit of the citation from Reinhard. I do not indeed hold it advisable for a man to spend his whole life in enquiring whether he can pick holes in his own faith, as such a temper will inevitably be unfavourable to any elevation of purpose—any high improvement of himself or others. I think, however, that every teacher of religion is bound to ' *keep his mind always open* to every better conviction of religion;' but I think also, that if, after due and full and fair enquiry, he finds himself in an entire state of disbelief of the doctrines which he has formerly subscribed, he is bound to relinquish his situation as teacher in the Church which professes those doctrines, and *has employed him only because he did so too.*

* Translation, p. 46.

Apostles and early Fathers of the Church. I have forgotten, he says, that the English Church was reformed because Henry VIII. wished to get rid of his wife! Poor Dr. Bretschneider! and poor Rationalists!—But the appeal to the Fathers is a mortal sin in his eyes; and he accuses * not me only, but the whole Church of England in early times, of considering the Fathers of the first century as a sort of second Bible; and he is quite sure that I have neither read the Fathers, nor can I know any thing about them, when I thus appeal to them; for—mark, reader, this fresh specimen of Dr. Bretschneider's logic, and his delicate compliment to me,—they are full of absurd opinions and errors! And he very wisely devotes four or five pages † to show that Barnabas says that Christ chose the worst men for his disciples; —that Hermas promises Revelations to those that fast;—that the Fathers of the three first centuries adopted the allegorical style of interpretation, and other absurdities, &c.—and then triumphantly asks, Does Mr. Rose agree with the Fathers in all these follies? His ingenious argument amounts to this:—You recommend our referring to the Fathers as witnesses to matters of fact. The Fathers talk a great deal of nonsense. If you had

* Translation, p. 46.   † Ibid. pp. 47—52.

read them and known this, you would not have so
referred to them.   Therefore you have never
read them ! What is one to say, I must again ask,
to such a reasoner ? Simply, I think, to beg that
he will try at least to understand the passage
which he has quoted from the Formula Concordiæ,
and in which the German Reformers state in what
light they use early creeds and writings—namely,
as *witnesses.*   If I were to dispute with Dr. Bretschneider, for example, on the Divinity of our
Lord, and he denied my interpretation of Scripture, is it not competent to me to say, ' the early
Christian writers understood Scripture as I do,'
without becoming responsible for their blunders * ?

---

* It will hardly be believed that Dr. Bretschneider, who *does*
profess to have read the Fathers, gives the result of his study as
follows :—' The Fathers of the three first centuries knew nothing
of the doctrine of the Trinity, of original sin, of men's inability
to do what is right, of the satisfaction of Christ ! They had no
developed idea of the reconciling efficacy of the death of Christ,
and considered baptism as the sacrament in which only *previous
sins* were forgiven, while man *himself was to atone for subsequent
ones,* held various opinions as to the origin of evil, and had an
infinity of superstitions as to demons, angels, the millennium,
&c. Such are the witnesses to whom Mr. Rose appeals as the
best interpreters of a Divine Revelation, and of the meaning of
the Bible.' Such are the views of a person defending a party
which professes to read without prejudice, and to judge with im-
partiality !

Are these Dr. Bretschneider's notions of the study of history ?—He concludes his section on the Fathers with a gross misconception of my meaning. Having recommended an appeal to the writings of the early Fathers as *witnesses*, I say,

' This then is the state of things on the hypothesis of a Divine Revelation; truth was as clearly revealed at the outset of Christianity, as it ever was intended to be known; its record is in Scripture; and if doubt as to the meaning of Scripture with respect to doctrine occurs, we can appeal to witnesses competent from the time when they lived, and the knowledge they must have enjoyed, to remove those doubts entirely. Where then is earthly philosophy? It is excluded. There is no scope under such a system for its discoveries,' &c.

This, Dr. Bretschneider (*not* the Translator) makes * into a statement, that ' in the first Church there was no room for philosophy ;' and then goes on to shew, that all the early Fathers attempted to apply the philosophy of the day to Christianity! He ought at least to be contented with my Translator's dishonesty, and not to add perversions of his own.

* Translation, p. 53.

G

In the course of my work, I have stated, that Semler and many of the Rationalists expunge large portions of Scripture from the canon; to which Dr. B. answers *, that the same was done in the early centuries. I never complained of Semler for ejecting any portion of Scripture from the canon, but *for doing so on bad grounds*. Unless he thought a writing *useful,* he said it could not be divine, and then he wished it ejected. What answer to this is it to say, that in the beginning of the fifth century, certain of the Epistles and the Revelation were reckoned of dubious authenticity?

Next †, because I do not think the Rationalists' idea of correcting and perfecting Christianity a very wise one, I am told, that there was something very similar in the three first centuries, when a great difference was made between the faith of the intellectual and that of the vulgar! When I complain that the Rationalists reject miracles, I am told ‡, that Luther talked of them as only fit for the ignorant and vulgar, as apples and pears are for children; and that Quenstedt, Calov, and others §, whom I praise, said that miracles require

---

* Translation, p. 55.   † Ibid. p. 56.   ‡ Ibid. p. 57.

§ Dr. B. obviously does gross injustice to these persons, when he says, from these declarations, that they thought the miracles only *fides humana,* while the true miracles, the inward workings of Christianity on the heart, require a *fides divina!* When I complain of the indifference to religion in Germany, (which Dr. B. does not deny,—indeed he could not, as he wrote a book on the subject himself,—but which he says is dying away,) I am told, that Origen complains of the same thing in his own times; whence, by some singular process of reasoning, Dr. B. concludes, that the present indifference in Germany does not proceed from the Rationalist doctrines, and that I am therefore very much in the wrong, and the Rationalists very much in the right! After settling this, much to his own satisfaction, (I may add, with great truth, and to mine also,) he proceeds to prove *, that I am not only foolish and ignorant in general, but especially ignorant of German theology. To speak seriously, I

only intended for the contemporaries of Christ. They neither said nor thought so. Their distinction as to the two kinds of faith is perfectly intelligible. No one ever thought the miracles more than external proofs of the truth. They are not the practical amenders of the heart, nor as such intended to be the *highest* objects of faith. With respect to Luther, every allowance is to be made for careless expressions in his works. A warm temper, haste, persecution, and slander, will excuse many improprieties of phrase. I have not Luther's works at hand, so as to know whether he is fairly represented in this quotation.

* Translation, p. 59, and following.

had hoped from a person like Dr. B., some correc-
tions, in this part of his work, of such errors as
very probably might have found their way into
one like mine. I should readily have received,
nay, I should have been thankful for such correc-
tions. I was aware that I had taken all the means
in my power to gain information, and all possible
diligence to represent every thing fairly, but still,
as I have said before, a foreigner is always liable
to fall into errors in going into so extensive a
subject. Let us see then what Dr. B. charges as
the extent of mine. First, he says, that I have
thrown all the opinions differing from the orthodox ones together, when in fact there are four
distinct sets of such opinions. Now the fact is,
that I carefully and distinctly state *, that I do not
seek to do more than indicate the general tendency
of the sentiments of the Rationalists, and that the
full extent of the opinions of which I complain,
is not held by *all* the divines of whom I speak.
By what right then does Dr. B. bring this unjust
accusation against me ? I might ask, with equal
truth, whether there is any real foundation for
his formal classification,—whether almost all the
Rationalists (I except perhaps one or two fana-
tics) did not set out from the same *principles,*

* Translation, p. 70.

and travel along the same road, the only difference between them being that some went a little
farther and some stopped short *.

Wegscheider, in speaking of Rationalism and
Rationalists, § 9, 10, 11, 12, makes no formal division, but, like myself, treats the Rationalists as
guided by one principle, but 'vario modo rece-
dentes' from Supernaturalism. And in a MS account of the Neologist school, lately put into my
hands, drawn up by a Socinian of considerable
abilities and learning, (resident for some time at

---

* The Rationalist principle as to Revelation in one word is
this, that we are not after the old fashion,—first to enquire whether what professes to be an immediate Revelation from God is
really so, and then entirely to submit ourselves to the doctrines
it contains, but that we are to begin by enquiring into the doctrines it contains, and ascertaining whether they are agreeable to
our (miserably imperfect and shallow) conceptions of what a Revelation ought to be. The difference between the various classes
of Rationalists has arisen from their own inconsistency. Assuming this as their principle, some timid spirits have, nevertheless,
been afraid of pursuing it to its full consequences, and have endeavoured to patch on here and there a positive doctrine to their
scanty creed. Such men are, perhaps, hardly less mischievous,
and assuredly they are more contemptible, than the bolder members of the party, who, having convinced themselves of the truth
of their principle, follow it wherever it leads them, *per fas et
nefas.*

Göttingen) the following observation occurs :—
' All did not go equally far : there was a distinction made of Rationalists, and Naturalists, which
appear however to me degrees only of the same
thing.' However, I am quite willing to give my
readers the benefit of Dr. B.'s classification, begging them to observe, that he *omits* all notice of
the most prominent writers in his classes, and
begging them also to observe the statements
made as to the condition of German theology
since 1750, by one of the Rationalizing divines.

The *first* class *, says Dr. B., considered Revelation as a superstition, and Jesus either as an
enthusiast or a deceiver. To this class belong
Wünsch and Paalzow, but *no divine*. I have myself said †, that *few* writers attacked our Saviour's
character ; but, be it remembered, that I have
cited books where he was treated at all events as
an enthusiast, and that Bahrdt himself, originally
a divine, goes farther still.

The second class does not allow that there was
any *divine* operation as to Christianity in *any* way,
and refers the origin of Christianity to mere natural causes. They make the life of Christ a
romance, and him a member of secret associa-

* Translation, p. 60.　　　　† Ibid. p. 80.

tions, and consider the Scriptures as only human writings, in which the word of God is not to be found. To this class belong Bahrdt, Reimarus, and Venturini, (the two last *not* divines), and perhaps Brennecke.

The third class comprises the persons usually called Rationalists. They acknowledge, in Christianity, an institution divine, beneficent, and for the good of the world, and Jesus as a messenger of God, and they think that in Scripture is found a true and eternal word of God,—only they deny *any supernatural and miraculous* working of God, and make the object of Christianity to be the introduction of religion into the world, its preservation and extension, and they distinguish between what is essential and non-essential in Christianity, between what is local and temporal, and what is universal. That is to say, they allow that there is good in Christianity—that all that is good comes from God; and, therefore, that Christianity comes from God: but miracles, inspiration, every thing *immediately* coming from God, they wholly disbelieve. Among this class, Mr. B. reckons Kant, Steinbart, Krug, as philosophers; and as divines, W. A. Teller, Löffler, Thiess, Henke, J. E. C. Schmidt, De Wette, Paulus, Wegscheider, and Röhr.

Last of all comes the fourth class *, which goes a little higher, and (as Dr. B. says) considers the Bible and Christianity as a divine Revelation in a higher sense than the Rationalists; assumes a revealing operation of God distinguishable from his common providence, carefully distinguishes the periods of this divine direction, founds the divinity of Christianity more on its internal evidence than on miracles, but especially separates Church-belief † from the doctrines of Scripture, reforms it according to the sentiments of the Divine Word, and requires that reason should try Revelation, and that Revelation should contain nothing *against*, though it may well have much *above* reason.   Döderlein, Morus, Reinhard ‡ did,

---

* Translation, p. 62.

† This perpetual confusion is most extraordinary.   Church-belief, as Dr. B. calls it, is a setting forth of Scripture doctrines, as the composer of the form believes them to exist in Scripture. They may be rightly or wrongly set forth, but they still profess to be a mere *setting forth* of Scripture doctrines.   Dr. B. says, he and his party adhere to Scripture.   If they are asked, do you then believe that Christ is said to be God in Scripture? he must answer either yes or no; and, as soon as he has done so, he too is a setter forth of Scripture doctrines.

‡ I beg the reader to refer to the note in p. 77.—What will he think of Dr. B.'s honesty when he reads the following extract from Reinhard? ' I could not dissemble from myself,' says he, ' that to be consistent, one must adhere *exclusively either to rea-*

and Ammon, Schott, Niemeyer, Bretschneider, and others do, belong to this class.

Such is Dr. Bretschneider's view of things in Germany. Let me repeat, not only that I have stated the existence of differences generally, but that I have in some cases actually pointed out what Dr. B. has done. For example, I have stated that Döderlein (though not always quite consistent) held higher notions as to Scripture than many others. But passing this over, let me ask, whether Dr. B.'s statement in any degree shakes mine? Nay, let me ask, whether his statement is in any degree a fair one? The impression he wishes to convey is, that only *a few* of the theological writers in Germany have been violent, while the larger class

son or Scripture; that there are no consistent reasoners but the Deist and the partisan of Revelation.' He goes on to expose at great length the inconsistency of the Rationalists,—of those who attempt to unite the claims of reason and Revelation *to authority,* and to point out the evils arising from this plan in Germany. Then he says, ' that he saw that there was no plan for him but either to adhere firmly to natural religion, and reject the Gospel and all divine Revelation; or to attach himself as firmly to the system of Revelation, and *to make reason subordinate to Scripture in matters of faith.*' He next states his long attachment to Revelation, and concludes with saying, that ' he had no choice ; he was compelled to embrace the side of Revelation, and *admit all which could be proved by Scripture.*'— Reinhard, Lettres, p 99—106.

has held the mild opinions which he professes to
hold himself. To both these points I have a little
to say. First, let any one refer, not to my work,
but to Winer's Handbuch, to Enslin's Bibliotheca,
or I might say, to any tolerable German Catalogue;
let him remark who are the most voluminous
among the theological writers, and then let him
ask, how it is that in Dr. B.'s studied and formal
enumeration nine-tenths of these are omitted?
What Dr. B.'s motives for omitting them might
be, I have no right to say; but this I will state
without fear of contradiction, that had he noticed
them he must have altered his statements. What
could Dr. B. say—to select a few out of many—
of Bauer, and Dathe, and Vater, and Gabler, and
Augusti, and Eckermann, and Tieftrunk, and the
early writings of Kaiser, and others? If he will
meet me on this ground, if he will prove that the
authors I have referred to, and many others whom
I have passed over, are not *violent* Rationalists,
he will indeed benefit his cause. But on this
material point he is silent, wholly silent. He
insinuates that I have exaggerated the numbers,
and distorted the opinions of the Rationalists, and
then in a studied and formal enumeration, made
expressly to refute my statements, he drops all
mention of the majority of these writers, of the
most voluminous and the most violent. But,

next, he is anxious to have it believed that his own opinions, which he states are the prevalent ones, are of a different order from those of Wegscheider and the more violent writers. Why does he not tell us what his opinions are? How easy would it be, instead of mystifying the reader by speaking of a revealing activity of God, to say, that he believes Christianity either to be a revelation or not, that he conceives Christ to have been either a Moral Teacher, or a Divine Messenger, or a Divine Being, as the case may be, and that he accepts or rejects the doctrine of the atonement made for sin by the death of Christ? But there is not a word said, beyond those I have quoted, to enable us to decide how high or how low in the scale of Rationalism he stands. He classes himself with Ammon; and it is not very difficult to tell what that writer's opinions *were* *. Let any person refer, for example, to the citations I have made from his writings, and say what they think of his Christianity. Let them, while they have Dr. B.'s declaration, that Ammon, like himself, considers Scripture as a revelation in a higher sense than other Rationalists do, fresh in their mind, read the following additional extract from Ammon's Preface to the 5th Edition of Ernesti's Institutio:

* See ch. V.

'It is easy to understand that pious and good men, who refer all events to God, would write especially of the commencement of a new religion, so as to have the will, works, and decrees of the Deity perpetually before them; an observation, the truth of which every page of the New Testament attests. In explaining these narrations, it is the duty of an interpreter not only to translate the words of the writer, but to give the clear sense of what he says, to refer effects to their causes, confine events by proper laws *, and by this strong mark distinguish *traditions* from *narrations,* and *dreams* from *facts.* It is not sufficient to remark, on Matt. iii. 17, that a voice was sent from heaven at the baptism of Jesus. "Adde potius e loco parallelo, Joh. xii. 29. βροντὴν γεγονέναι, &c. de liquido, cui suam quivis sententiam, ceu oraculo divino, substernere solebat." So, on Acts ix. 4, where it is said that Paul talked with Jesus from the clouds, a good interpreter will appeal to a place of clearly similar meaning, xxii. 17, where it is plainly said, " that the Apostle, being in an ecstasy, spoke with Jesus." If this right is denied us in explaining Scripture, why

---

* The Latin words are *eventa legibus ideoneis alliget*, which may be, *confine events to proper laws;* but Ammon's Latin is fearfully bad, as well as Wegscheider's.

do we try to explain it? why not suffer every
one in reading Scripture to be wise or foolish as
he will? why do we not leave it to any one to fill
it with figments, allegories, and other fanatical
opinions?'

Need I add any more on this point?

But Dr. B. follows these remarks with another
of great truth in itself, but not applicable here.
He says *, that it is not fair to judge of an age by
the opinions that pass through it, but by those
which it finally adopts and adheres to. And he
adds †, that there are four classes of opinions
which have been presented to the German public. (1.) Suppositions and hypotheses of learned
men, attacked as soon as published, and since forgotten: for example, those of the writer of *Horus*,
Bahrdt, Venturini, Reimarus, Eck, Brennecke,
&c. with many of Semler. (2.) Hypotheses which
gained for a time a good deal of applause and cur-
rency, but were still much opposed, and are either
now given up, or only held by few: as, for example, the *moral* interpretation of Scripture, (he
means Kant's) the explaining it in a modern
sense, the theory of accommodation in its greater

* Translation, p. 65.   † Ibid. p. 66.

extent, the natural explanation of miracles, &c.
(3.) Views which have gained reception, but only
with the smaller part of theologians: as the peculiar system of *Rationalism,* as set forth by Röhr
and Wegscheider; and (4.) Views such as are
held by himself, (and described above,) and, as he
says, by the greater part of the *Clergy* and *Laity.*
These alone have, according to Bretschneider,
found any resting-place in public opinion, and of
these, therefore, alone ought I to have spoken.
Now this inference I deny altogether. For the
last thirty or forty years, by his own confession,
all sorts of wild and absurd opinions have been
openly taught by very many writers of credit,
and in the German Protestant Churches some of
them are still retained; while in other quarters,
a less violent but still most material declination
from the ancient belief of the Lutheran and Cal-
vinist Churches has prevailed. That there may
be a tendency in both parties to relinquish the
more obnoxious part of their opinions,—that is
to say, that a fresh change of views may have
taken place, I am not concerned to deny. Now
it is all this precisely which I have stated; it is
this which appeared to me to present a most
striking and instructive lesson to us. What indeed can be more striking than to see the Ministers of a Church, Professors of Divinity, &c. &c.,

throwing about, as if in sport, opinions, either subversive entirely of Christianity, or reducing it to mere Socinianism, and setting at defiance the Church to which they belong? Why it is unfair and improper to state what has been thus going on, I am at a loss to understand. It may be perfectly true that the most violent opinions are declining. What is violent seldom lasts; and I have too firm a reliance on God's providential care for his Church, to believe that he will not find a remedy for this mischief. But it is not the less true that the mischief *has* existed, and it is not the less advisable to inquire into its cause, and profit by the lesson which the inquiry gives. But let me ask most of all, whether Dr. Bretschneider's opinions are not such as to justify me in the eyes of all Christians above Socinianism. I have no wish to argue who is right or who is wrong, but I wish to ask, whether Dr. Bretschneider believes Jesus to be a Divine person, whether he believes that our justification is procured through his death, and that our sanctification is the work of the Holy Spirit. Let him answer these questions in the sense in which he knows they are put, and if his answers be in the affirmative, I will certainly retract with respect to his party.

Last of all, Dr. B*. attacks the sources from which he is pleased to think I have derived my information. I happened in my Preface to mention as *convenient* books, a slight sketch by Tittman, Schröckh's History, a work of Bahrdt's, and Wegscheider's well-known volume ; and I added, that as I could not get in this country some of the OLDER works ' necessary for illustrating *the growth and progress*' of these opinions, I had FOR THEM (not for any others) referred to Ernesti's Theological Review. Dr. B. assumes very artfully, that these are my *only* written sources of information, and then he pronounces that Tittman's work is only a short *imperfect* account of a part of the subject †. I never said it was more ; nay, I mentioned that it was not well thought of, but that it was convenient as a compendium. But Ernesti's book is obsolete, says Dr. B ‡. and it is quite absurd to refer to it !

* Translation, p. 69.

† This censure as it stands in Dr. B's. work applies to Schröckh and not to Tittman,—but this I conceive to be a mere mistake in printing. The work he speaks of he describes as short, and coming down to the time of Kant. This applies to Tittman, whereas Schröckh has written one history in thirty-five, the other (since the Reformation,) in twelve volumes.

‡ Translation, p. 71.

Why, in the name of wonder ? Was Ernesti not learned and not candid ? Did he not represent fairly the opinions of the writers he reviewed *in his own day ?* I have appealed to him for nothing else.—Then ' Bahrdt's work is contemptible and long forgotten.' Be it so. I have no doubt that the Rationalists wish it forgotten ; but it is still, as I said, very convenient, for it is a systematic exposition of the Lutheran faith, with short notes below the text, stating the new opinions, so that reference can be made to any subject at once. And the opinions briefly stated by Bahrdt are those of many of the Rationalists, repeated a thousand times in various works.—Are such books, asks Dr. B., sufficient to give a view of the progress and the present state of Rationalism * ? Certainly not ; and he cannot but be aware that I never pretended they were, but that in the notes I have referred to a *vast number* of authors for this purpose. Such an artifice is not worthy a person

---

* Dr. B. here very properly points my attention to the *periodical* works of Germany, a very important branch of their literature undoubtedly. It is curious enough that one of my English assailants, a Mr. Hett, imagines, with that perfect acquaintance with Germany for which our countrymen are so remarkable, that the German Journals are like our Monthly and London Magazines, and is extremely severe upon me for having referred to them so constantly.

of Dr. B.'s reputation.—He goes on to state,*, that in his opinion I have derived most of my knowledge from certain friends of mine, Anti-Rationalists, in Germany : and he subsequently alludes to *one.* Nay, one of the Journals † on his side of the question designates Professor Tholuck in particular as my informant. And the Translator of the Sermons in his preface brings forward the same charge, expressly stating, that it is impossible (good man !) that I should have myself gained all the information I have brought forward, an observation which perhaps I ought to consider as complimentary. However, in justice to Professor Tholuck, I beg to say, that I am not in any way acquainted with that gentleman, and never received the slightest communication from him. But I beg to make a still stronger statement, namely, that I received no assistance whatever from any friend, German or English, beyond that *actually stated* in the notes. As Dr. B. shamefully misrepresents that assistance, let us see to what it amounts. In pp. 115 and 117, I mention, that ' my knowledge as to the oath on going into orders, was derived from Germans on whom I

* Translation, pp. 71, 72.

† The Allgemeine Kirchenzeitung for Thursday, Oct. 12, 1826, and the Appendix to it, called Theologisches Literatur-blatt, for Friday, Dec. 15. No. 100. p. 1809.

could depend.' It was so. I derived that information from a young Clergyman of the highest character, and a Layman of exalted learning, who has long paid especial attention to liturgical questions; both of whom I met *out* of Germany. But of their private opinions on religion I know nothing, and I should have offended against the decency of private intercourse if I had presumed to inquire. The friend mentioned in p. 161, is an English gentleman; and the persons referred to lower in that page, and in p. 162, were all *Laymen*, who gave me no *opinions* of their own, but merely spoke to *facts* which they had themselves known when studying in the Gymnasia. The information as to the incomes of the Clergy in the north of Germany, in p. 185, came from some English friends long resident at Dantzic; and finally, the friends spoken of in p. 166, were English friends. All farther assistance I beg entirely and positively to disclaim; so that all Dr. B.'s long dissertation, and his hope that my German friend, who has given me such a black picture of German theology, may see his answer to me, has been written in vain. Some part of it is indeed ridiculous in other respects. He says *, I have a very absurd *correspondent* in Germany,

---

* Translation, p. 72.

H 2

because I express, in p. 182, ' my sincere pleasure in knowing, that in Germany a better order of things may be expected. Some of the Rationalists have openly retracted—some are silent—the system is on the decline—and the new appointments to the theological chairs are made from a better class of thinkers and scholars.' What made him think of a correspondent, I know not. I was only repeating what I had stated elsewhere, on the authority of *printed* documents. And on the authority of those documents I beg to ask Dr. B. who says, that no one knows any thing of all this in Germany, whether he means to deny, for example, that Ammon has retracted?—that Kaiser has retracted?—that De Wette has retracted? Does Dr. B. indeed know nothing of this? If that is true, I, at least, am not answerable for his ignorance of what others know. But does he not know that there is a determination in the Governments to discourage the Rationalists, and appoint persons of different opinions to situations in the Universities and elsewhere? Does he indeed know nothing, for example, of an ordonnance of the Grand Duke of Baden against the Rationalists? Most assuredly he does. Even within the last few months, he knows of a contest with regard to this very Professor Tholuck, who has been seated in a fresh professorship, to the great discomfiture of the Rationalists.

But I have now a more serious matter to discuss with Dr. Bretschneider. I have said *, that ' I assert, on the faith of public and recorded as well as private testimonies, that these doctrines were publicly taught from the pulpit †. Nay, I have not seen any contradiction to this from any of the party themselves, except as to the generality of the usage. They allow its frequency,' &c. Dr. B. says, that no doubt these doctrines were taught in the lecture room, but ‡ that it is *untrue* that they were taught in the *pulpit* §. Now, in the year 1822, though he has forgotten it, he himself published a book, (Ueber die Unkirchlichkeit dieser Zeit,) in the 49th and 50th pages of which, he *admits* the fact which he now denies. He states there, that the change of religious opinions had great influence *on the sermons*, the books of religious instruction published

* Translation, p. 83.

† Dr. B. quotes this—' brought forward from the pulpit and the professor's chair.' The last clause is an addition of his own. It is of no consequence—but it is as well in a *direct* quotation to quote only what you find.

‡ Translation, p. 73.

§ Dr. B.'s strange logic here shows itself again. To prove that the Rationalist principles were not taught in sermons, he refers me to sermons where such doctrines are not taught. It were much to be desired, that he would learn the difference between negative and positive.

by the Clergy *for the young* and for the people, and that *many* preachers used these means to alter the people's opinions on religion. Within sixty years, says he, the sermons have altered very much, and in *contents, tone,* and *form,* have followed the spirit of the age! This needs no comment, or I could give a very ample one. Want of truth, no doubt there is, but whether with me or not, others may judge! After this specimen, I need hardly reply to his angry comment on my saying, that the neological doctrines were taught in the Gymnasia, and that the miracles were then spoken of with contempt. He says, that I cannot prove this to be *generally* true, and I have myself said, that my information was, of course, private. But I may observe, that he himself allows, that the change in opinions had great effect on the religious instruction given by the Clergy to the *young;* and I can only repeat what I have said, that from testimonies I cannot doubt, it was common for these doctrines to be taught both in the Gymnasia and in the preparation for confirmation. Dr. B. is very eloquent in his anger against me for this charge; but he must remember, that he only brings assertion against assertion. I cannot, too, but remark, in what a situation he himself places the Rationalists. That a large body of the Clergy went forth from the Universities imbued with the opinions of one or other of the classes of whom he has spoken, even he will not deny. If they did *not* teach the opinions they believed, what did they teach? Does he mean, that in their instructions to the young, (where they could not evade the point, as they might in the pulpit, by preaching morality founded on expediency,) they taught what they did not believe? Such is indeed the alternative to which their persisting to remain in a situation, for which their opinions unfitted them, must necessarily have reduced them. They must have been compelled either to enforce what they considered as falsehood, or to do what Dr. B. allows would have been dreadful, to impress opinions on the young, the poor, and the ignorant, which in them, at least, would most probably destroy every vestige of religion, and therefore of morality.

I have now concluded my notice of Dr. B.'s strictures. The task of examining them has been any thing but pleasant; for it has consisted, not in defending my principles, but in correcting the errors, and complaining of the evasions and perversions of my adversary. Yet it will not, I think, be labour entirely thrown away. On the one hand, the miserable defence which Dr. B. has offered for the Rationalists, is the best proof of

the state of their cause; on the other, I feel that
I may in future be fairly released from the necessity of noticing any attacks from Dr. Bretschneider.   It cannot be required that I should enter
into farther controversy with a writer, who, instead of a frank and open defence, meets me with
mere special pleading, and who neglects, or is ignorant of the common laws of courtesy.

V. DR. AMMON.

===

Die unveränderliche Einheit der Evangelische Kirche. Eine Zeitschrift von Dr. Christoph Friedrich von Ammon. Zweites Heft. Dresden, 1826.

I HAVE had the misfortune to give Dr. Ammon personal offence, in some degree by the epithets ' vain and rash,' which I could not refrain from applying to his early writings, but still more, I apprehend, by speaking of his Latinity as barbarous.   This last is an offence which he cannot forgive ; he threatened me with castigation in his first number, and the storm has broken in ten very atrabilious pages in the second.   I regret this unfeignedly, for although Dr. Ammon is far from a powerful writer, he is now, I believe, a right-minded one, and he and I are fighting on the same side of the question.   But Dr. Ammon's situation is a very peculiar one, and may, to some persons, account for his loss of temper.   He set out in life as a violent Rationalist.   He is now shocked at these opinions, and denounces them with the same eagerness with which he once espoused them, and with that warmth which occasionally distinguishes the exertions of converts and proselytes. His zeal in his new cause, his attacks and his sarcasms on his old friends, have, as it may easily be supposed, not excited any very pleasant feelings in their minds. And they occasionally hint at his change of opinions in a way against which Dr. Ammon's temper is not proof. As he is not any longer a young man, it is somewhat strange that lapse of time has not taught him that the gods do not grant all things to one man. To hold violent opinions and to renounce them is a good deal; but to reproach and revile those who still persevere in them, and to expect that they will receive the attack in patient silence, is rather too much. To renounce error under honest conviction is wise, right, and honourable; nor can there be any reason why the convert should not openly oppose what he once openly and wrongly defended. But he should do it in temperance, in candour, and in charity *.

---

* Dr. Ammon, I apprehend, alludes to his own case in the following remarks, which I find in a prefatory essay, prefixed to the first number of the Unver. Einheit, and intended to explain its views. After observing, that it is not right to draw any inferences against the unity of the Church from errors and a spirit of sectarianism prevailing in it, (a pretty strong doctrine) because as weeds grow up among corn, so the seeds of unbelief and false reasoning spring up perpetually in the human heart, he goes on thus. ' If then Protestant writers have produced doctrines irreconcilable with

These plain truths Dr. Ammon forgets, and is angry beyond measure, when any of his former friends complain of him. He has, for example, appropriated (I believe very rightly) some remarks made by Dr. Tzschirner on persons who, ' *though the light has broken on them late enough*, are for ever painting the new theology in the blackest colours, venting miserable witticisms on its defenders, and representing the variety of opinions in the Protestant Church as a serious evil *.' And

the foundations of their Church, they did it out of their order, *nay, against their oath and their duty*, and their apology must be, that they acted either from a love of scribbling and from precipitancy, or from the proper wish to spread the reign of truth. And not only will candour and knowledge of human nature justify this second supposition, but it is strengthened by observing, that the bolder Naturalists never left the Church, nay, even defended it against its enemies. If these men are now truly Christian teachers in heart and spirit, we may say of them as of Augustine and Luther, that in their riper years they voluntarily brought themselves into the spirit of their Church, and that, like St. Paul, they now defend that truth which they before denied or attacked.' (Unveränd. Einh. Pt. I. p. 36.) In several places he recognises *the necessity of creeds*, and (p. 55.) he says, that one end of his work is to show, that ' if Reason forgets that she must learn from God and thence unboldens herself to judge of his holy word, she must be put under the authority of faith, for the *dignity of Jesus and the divinity of his Gospel are not consistent with Rationalism*.'

* Dr. Ammon's reply does not do much credit to his candour. Dr. Tzschirner, a *liberal* Protestant, twenty years ago praised a

he is very angry with Dr. Tzschirner for thus ranging himself, as he says, ' on Vicar Rose's side!' He would show both his good sense, his candour, and his Christian disposition far more, by bearing in patience those statements of his former opinions and his change, which are strictly true, and which, if he had the right feeling to see it, can now do him no discredit, but must rather tend to exalt his character.   He judges differently, however, it would seem, and is worked into absolute frenzy by Dr. Tzschirner's and my allusions to his early Rationalism and his conversion *, though I at least, so far from blaming, praised his renunciation of his error.   That and the charge against his Latin are too bad to bear. And accordingly he attacks me most furiously, although we are so much agreed against the Rationalists, that I might almost make my strongest statements in his words.   What, for

work of Ammon's (then a liberal Protestant too) as agreeing with Scripture, and showing the possibility of an union of Reason and Revelation.   Dr. Ammon having changed his opinions, quotes this commendation as proving Dr. Tzschirner's inconsistency in attacking him now.   Dr. Ammon ought to remember, that as his opinions have altered, so has he altered every edition of the work alluded to !

* There is a very severe and stinging note on this subject, levelled at some individual, perhaps Dr. A., by the Translator of my Sermons, p. 108.

example, is his reply to Tzschirner, who, like other Rationalists, thinks unity even in essentials of no consequence, and says, that it is enough to believe ' that in the Gospel, God proclaims himself as not only a righteous judge, but as rich in grace, and merciful; that Christ is the Saviour of the world, and brings men to God; and that the hope of pardon lies, and can alone be found, in a heart-renewing and sanctifying faith in the merciful One in heaven, whom the Saviour of the world has revealed,' Dr. Ammon, as an old Rationalist, well knowing that these fine words mean nothing, makes the following admirable answer. ' Yet among many opinions, one only can be true; yet we ought to acknowledge the pure full truth which frees us from the dominion of opinions; yet the aim of our endeavours ought to be, not the imperfection which, by human frailty, can scarcely be avoided, but a fullness and unity of knowledge; yet we ought to hold fast at least to the essential truths of salvation, and not to say that it is a matter of indifference whether God is one with the world or not—whether his decree to make us happy, is absolute, or dependent on his wisdom and love—whether Christ was a man like Luther, or the Son of God—*whether he is the Saviour of the world only as a Teacher, or as a Mediator*; yet we ought to place our hope for pardon not only in that trust in a merciful Judge, which is the trust of Judaism and Islamism, but in a faith in our justification before God through Jesus, as the Epistle to the Romans clearly shews, and the deep and inward connection of the Christian scheme of salvation requires.   A hope for mercy from a merciful judge, preceded by no justification of the converted sinner, destroys, as Melanchthon has clearly proved, not only all the Christian system of atonement, and the first distinguishing tenet of our Church, but the holiness of the moral government of the world,' &c. After going on in the same strain at some length, and enquiring why, if doctrines are of such little matter, and if a mere wish to promote a knowledge of God, virtue, and morality be enough, Deists or Unitarians should not be received into Church-communion, he ends with saying, ' Human reason is inclined to unite all the religions of the earth by generalization, but it is exactly by this abstraction, that the essence of Christianity is lost as a peculiar revelation ; the essence of the Evangelical Church disappears with its positive and well-grounded dogmas ; the organic unity of faith and essential doctrines without which no Church can exist, is gone ; and we see, when it is too late, that not our foundation, but that which has been laid for us by God is the only true and tenable one.'   Some of these words

are almost my own *, and I could not desire to
have used any clearer or more decisive ones.
When I add to this, that Dr. Ammon now acknowledges the necessity of a decided *creed*,
talks of the power of the oath of the clergy, &c.
&c. the reader will easily see that it is not difference of opinion, but personal pique, which has
provoked Dr. Ammon to display such a sad want
of common candour, and so entire a loss of temper
and decency in writing against me. He is, indeed,
so sensitive on the point of his former opinions,
that he cannot bear any one except himself to
speak against them. A writer whom he notices
in the subsequent pages of his journal, and who,
like myself, attributes to the violence of the Rationalists many conversions to the Roman Catholic Church, is attacked by Dr. Ammon for this
very reason with the greatest asperity.

One word more I may be allowed to say on Dr.
Ammon's present opinions. He is, I trust, too honest to use words, like his old friends the Rationalists, in an ambiguous sense. We may then surely
understand from the passage I have quoted, that he
now believes in the Divinity of our Lord, and
in justification through his blood. And in other
places † he declares clearly his faith in the mira-

---

* See pp. 34, 35.   † Part I. p. 66.

cles of Jesus and his Apostles. Yet he has not joined what we should call the orthodox party; but designates their belief* as pseudo-orthodoxical Palæology †. Dr. Bretschneider too, who would never venture to assert *his own* belief in the Divinity of Jesus, or the justification of man through his blood, claims Dr. Ammon for his own; and both in the attack on me, and elsewhere, Dr. A. speaks of prophecies and of miracles, (in which, as I have just stated, he now professes to believe,) not indeed in his former tone, but still in a tone any thing but decent and proper, as will be seen below ‡. These contradictions I notice, but do not attempt in any way to explain.

But it is time for me to leave these general matters, and to notice the charges advanced by Dr. Ammon against my work.

I cannot say, as Hooker did, that my adversary's reply consists of railings and reasons, but of railings and sophisms, or falsehoods. To the railings I shall certainly say nothing; to the sophisms I regret that I must waste my time in saying the few words that follow.

---

* P. 54.   † Part I. p. 55.   ‡ See p. 121.

His account of the objects of my work is fair enough, while he refers to chapter and verse; but he concludes it with saying, that one of my especial declarations is, that the Bible is treated with contempt in Germany; that the German divines dedicate themselves to divinity, without any previous classical acquirements; and that I complain bitterly of the German style of explaining prophecies and wonders. For these statements he makes no reference to my work, for the very simple reason, that out of these three allegations two are entirely false. I never said that the Bible is treated with contempt in Germany*. Though I should not have gone far from the truth in saying, that they who think the sacred writers weak, or ignorant, or fraudulent, who think that some prophecies were made after the event, and that some miracles were trick, and who think that all the positive doctrines of Christianity were local and temporary, treated the Bible with contempt, I did not say it even of them; far less was I rash or violent enough to say, that the Bible was so treated in Germany at large. Dr. Ammon has therefore on this point asserted a direct and injurious falsehood.

Again, I never said, that the German divines

---

* This accusation Dr. A. repeats in pp. 49, 50.

had no knowledge of classical literature.   In fact
I said nearly the contrary,—when I state, in speaking of Paullus and others, that they were learned
men as far as reading and collecting could make
them so.   What I really said was, that they were
not scholars *of a high order ;* and I regretted that
the really illustrious scholars of Germany, the Her-
manns, the Böckhs, the Thierschs, the Welckers,
and the Buttmans, did not occasionally at least
turn from the pages of profane literature, to shed
the light of their great talents and profound learning on the interpretation of Scripture.   Had they
done so, the weak and perverse trash with which
Scripture has been depraved and polluted by some
of the Rationalists, would never have been heard
of, and one source of mischief would have been
entirely stopped.   These perversions of my words
are disgraceful.

Dr. Ammon, like my other antagonists, next tries
to get rid of my accusation by recriminating on
the Church of England.   The folly with which
he does so, it would not be easy to match.   Mr.
Sheridan, he says, once wrote a satirical sermon
for a Bishop who was dining with him, and the
Bishop preached it the next Sunday !   And besides this, an Atheistical English Bishop once
travelled on the continent.   Such things could

not happen in the German Church, though Mr. Rose says, there is so little controul in it over the Clergy!

Whether the story of Mr. Sheridan be true or not, it is not worth while to enquire; but in what a state must that man's understanding be, who would draw inferences as to the condition of a Church, because it had at one time a mad Bishop, and at another a foolish one! nay! more,—who could think such charges against another Church any defence of his own!

The next thing worth notice is, Dr. Ammon's exceeding anger about his Latin. He wishes his readers to believe, that part of my charge against the Rationalists is, that they write bad Latin. The fact is, that I noticed the matter only incidentally in a note, and simply because I was not always sure that I understood the strange semi-German, semi-Latin phraseology in which Ammon, Wegscheider, and others write, and was afraid I might misrepresent them. But Dr. Ammon enters into a long and laboured defence of his parts, and tells us, that solecisms have been found in Erasmus, Scaliger, &c., that some learned English have committed errors, and that a member of Parliament blundered in Aristænetus between Median and Medical.

Poor Dr. Ammon!   I am sorry he is so much distressed about his Latin, and still more sorry that he has nothing better to say for it.

He next seeks to convict me of positive errors. Those which he alleges are curious, and to me most satisfactory.   If these are the only errors his penetration can discover, I have not much cause for alarm.   The first is as follows : I said that ' these statements of Wegscheider are repeated by Ammon.'   Now the work of Wegscheider, to which I referred, was published in 1815, while Ammon's appeared in 1803. Dr. Ammon thinks, that by using the word *repeat*, I meant that he *copied* his statement from Wegscheider.   If I had, the matter would have been of little moment.   Which of two contemporary authors first made a statement *peculiar to neither, but found in many writers prior to both,* is really a point of so little importance, that there would be no great harm in not comparing the dates on their title-pages.   But the truth is, that I only meant that what was expressed in Wegscheider, is *also expressed* in Ammon.   I had said just before, in the same intention, ' all these views of Wegscheider are held by Ammon.'

Again, I have said, that Döderlein quotes Am-

mon's Christology, whereas, says Dr. A., Döderlein died in 1792, and Ammon's work appeared
only in 1794. The fact however is as I stated,
that (in the sixth edition of) Döderlein's work *,
Ammon's Christology is referred to. There are
two ways of cutting this knot. Döderlein may
have seen the work in MS, which is not impro-
bable, both because Ammon having been known
as an author certainly two years before Döderlein's death, and probably more, the similarity
of their opinions on many points might produce
a communication between them, and because no
particular page of the work is referred to. Or
the editor of Döderlein's work may have inserted
the reference. The only objection to the latter
supposition is, that he professes to *mark* all he
introduces, so that the reader may distinguish
between his additions and the original work, and
I can find no such mark attached to the passage
in which Ammon's work is quoted. If this latter
solution, however, as I am inclined to believe, is
the true one, I, no doubt, am in error; of the extent of that error the reader will judge.—It is
this,—I did not know the exact year in which
Döderlein died. That Ammon had been known
as a writer some years before Döderlein's death,

* Vol. ii. p. 221.

I was aware.' I saw one of Ammon's earliest
works quoted in one of Döderlein's latest, and
I certainly, therefore, did not suspect that it was
not quoted by Döderlein himself. Indeed, if I
had doubted, I had no means at hand of deciding
without an enquiry, which was not worth the trouble, how long after 1791 or before 1797 * Döderlein
died; and I should therefore probably have written as I did, under the same uncertainty as I now
am, whether Döderlein himself might have seen
Ammon's work in MS, and have noticed it in the
fifth edition, or even subsequently in his MS pre-
parations for a sixth. The matter was not one of
the slightest consequence; for the only fact still remains as it was stated, viz. that there is in Döderlein's work a reference to Ammon's. Accuracy,
however, and minute accuracy is no doubt desirable, and I must leave it to the reader to judge, whether this error convicts me of any serious want of
it. I rather wonder that Dr. Ammon's eagle eyes
did not discern a clerical error, by which, as I
now see, I wrote, in the tedium of transcribing,
the name of *Döderlein* for that of *Wegscheider,* in

---

* I mention these dates, because Professor Junge, who published the sixth edition of Döderlein's work, which is the one I
possess, in 1797, speaks of him as then dead; and he superin-
tended the publication of the fifth himself in 1791.

p. 126, line 11, an error by which Döderlein's life is protracted to 1817. Had Dr. A. not failed to perceive it, he might have sounded a still louder note of triumph.

In return for Dr. A.'s accusations of me, his next remark affords me ample grounds for one of a serious nature against himself. In his Preface to the fifth edition of Ernesti's Institutio, dated 1792, he has the singular modesty to lay it down on his own authority, (in a dissertation of a few pages, prefixed, too, to a work intended to give safe and right principles of Hermeneutics) that many of the miracles in the New Testament are no miracles at all. After observing this in one of my notes, and mentioning his strange explanation of several of the miracles, the last of which happened to be the death of Ananias and Sapphira, I added, ' let it be observed, that the vain and rash man who, without doubt or hesitation, proposed *this mass of folly and impiety,* has had also the sincerity to confess his shame for it, and that by God's grace he is now a pious and humble Christian.' How has Dr. Ammon stated this? Will the reader believe, that the following is a literal translation of what he gives as an extract from my work, and an answer to it. 'Ammon has been so sincere as to confess, that he is ashamed of his view of the history of Ananias and Sapphira, and that through God's grace he is now a pious and humble Christian!' This is his pretended extract. Now for his answer. ' In speaking of the history of Ananias, the business was to defend Peter against Voltaire, who had set this matter in the most hateful light, and there has never been a word said of a retractation.' This is no blunder—the translator is not here in fault ; but Dr. Ammon, in order to avoid what it seems he has the bad feeling to think an awkward question, has changed my assertion of the general change of his sentiments as to Rationalism, into an assertion that he has changed his opinion about the miracle of Ananias and Sapphira ! And then he denies that any such change has taken place ! Such conduct needs no comment *. When

---

* I cannot, even in charity, believe that such a proceeding could arise from error or oversight ; but if I wanted any confirmation of my judgment in this respect, I should find it in the very next article to that in which Dr. A. speaks of me. He is reviewing Professor Borger's work, De Mysticismo ; and he professes to give an analysis of the book. Professor Borger, in enumerating all the causes which have led to mysticism in Germany, considers *Rationalism* as a principal one. He gives a long account of the Rationalizing Theology, and adds, that the disgust which it caused produced a reaction, finally leading to Mysticism. Dr. Ammon very carefully copies all the other causes assigned by Borger, but *omits all notice of Rationalism.*

I said that Dr. Ammon had become a pious and humble Christian, I fear I went too far; he has indeed renounced his ancient opinions, but I see nothing at least of Christian candour about him. His present opinion about prophecies and miracles is, that ' the Old Testament is a constant prophecy of Christ; but that no particular prophecy of the Messiah can be pointed out, as by itself affording a full proof, without the explanation afforded by the facts of the New Testament; and that as to miracles, the Evangelical Christian believes with Augustine and Luther in two great miracles, that of creation and preservation in the physical, and that of redemption and sanctification in the moral; these great theologians consider all other miracles as trifling, and far below the others. Whether Jesus walked on or in the sea; whether madness or the evil spirit was in the swine; whether Peter's fish had a new-stamped stater in his mouth, or an unstamped one, is of little, very little consequence; only an exegetical coxcomb can fear any danger from this quarter to his puny soul.' This method of speaking of the miracles appears to me neither decent nor

He cannot bring himself, even now, to allow any one else to state that the very opinions, which he has renounced, were mischievous, and has recourse to the most disingenuous proceedings in order to avoid these declarations.

sensible. It is true, doubtless, that the miracles addressed to our senses are intended only as *means* of faith; it is true, too, that the great wonders of creation and redemption produce a rapture and a reverence *in the Christian heart* which cannot be excited by the lesser manifestations of miraculous power. But it is true, too, that One wiser than we are, and who knew well what was in man, judged that these addresses to the senses were necessary to arouse a large portion of mankind, lost in the occupations or enjoyments of sense, to accept the doctrine to which they gave such unquestionable testimony, and thus to bring them by degrees to a better and higher state of mind. It is true, therefore, that without them, the wonders of redemption at least, would have remained, nay, would still remain unknown to a large portion of the world; and under the influence of that consideration alone, no right-minded man would speak of them lightly or irreverently, even if he felt no want of them to confirm his own faith, or elevate his own views.

The conclusion of Dr. Ammon's remarks is the only thing, I can safely say, in the whole of my opponents' attacks which has excited any other feeling than that of weariness and contempt. But however false and base his insinuation is, it has, I confess, moved my indignation. He says, that I returned to England 'from the arms of German hospitality,' to abuse and vilify German writers. Dr. Ammon's rage is so unbounded that he seizes the first argument which offers itself, however improper or false, to injure me. It is true, I did receive much kindness in Germany; the hours which I was allowed to spend with some of the most eminent German scholars will ever live in my remembrance; and if the praise of one so obscure and insignificant as I am could be of any avail, I am ready on all occasions to testify, as I have already done, my sincere and profound admiration of the genius and learning which exalt Germany to so high a place among the nations of the civilized world. These are feelings, indeed, which must be entertained by every candid man who is at all acquainted with the *extent* of research in Germany, and who compares it with that displayed in other countries. But I have yet to learn that Germany or any other country is perfect. I have yet to learn that the laws of honour or of good feeling bind the traveller to approve all he sees in a foreign country, or to declare his disapprobation when he leaves it. If such absurdities be tolerated, foreign travel must be abandoned as a source of reflection or improvement. But even Dr. Ammon's feeble mind

8

cannot be open to such folly. It is his malignity which has induced him to insinuate what is utterly false, that I *abused* German hospitality. If I had retailed private anecdotes, if I had spoken of the opinions of individuals, nay, still farther, if I had sought private confidence, and made use of the information so obtained, I should deserve not only Dr. Ammon's rebuke, (that is of little moment to me or to any man) but the contempt and indignation of every honourable mind. But I have not done so. I went into Germany for purposes of health, and not to study German divinity. My introductions were to scholars, and not to divines ; and they who take the trouble to look into my book will see that I refer to *printed works,* not to my own observations, and not to information obtained from any individual, except in one or two cases in speaking of points ' which might be proclaimed at Charing Cross.' In one word, I sought no private confidence and I have abused none. When my friends in Germany accuse me, Dr. Ammon has my full leave to take up the cry ; till then, he ought in common decency to abstain from accusations which are directed wholly against personal character, and which are utterly without foundation.

Having thus noticed all Dr. A.'s criminations, I

must go on to lay before my readers certain admissions which he has made in favour of my statements, and thus to extract what good I can from his evil.

He allows * that my work has found here and there approval in Germany from persons *of congenial opinions* to mine; he repeats this statement in page 52; and in page 54 he hints that some of them have even done me the honour of speaking of me as a fellow-writer in the cause of real Christianity. He admits † that I certainly might find ' often enough' in the works of German divines, the most absurd claims made for the rights of reason; that ‡ the plan pursued in the German Church, has sometimes, through ill-timed liberalism, favoured Anti-Christianism; that it would be better for the German clergy to read the Bible and the Fathers rather than fugitive journals as they do; and § that the Rationalists in talking of the perfectibility of Christianity, fell into the grossest error, as they confounded the mutability of their subjective knowledge with the immutability of divine truth. It is pretty clear then, I must repeat, that had I not unluckily affronted Dr. Ammon

* Page 45.   † Page 47.
‡ Page 48.   § Page 49.

about his Latin, his story and mine would not have been very different. I am happy to add, in conclusion, from a part of his critique on two works on Mysticism, his testimony against Rationalism, a testimony the more valuable as coming from one who knows it so well. ' Mysticism,' says he *, ' has this single merit, as every evil has some accompanying good, that it acts as a counterpoise to *Rationalism, which dries up the heart, and her companion Unbelief,* and prevents the entire ruin of public worship and religious feeling.' And again †, ' pure Rationalistic Protestantism is as different from the Evangelical Protestantism of the sixteenth century, as Natural Religion is from Christianity.'

---

* Page 67.   † Page 101.

VI. DR. BECK.

Allgemeines Repertorium, (1.) Vol. i. p. 285, *for* 1826 ; *and* (2.) Vol. i. p. 28, *for* 1827.

I NOTICE these articles for form's sake, that I may not be suspected of passing over any of the attacks on my work. The Allgem. Repertorium is a sort of epitome of all new works, and hardly pretends to any criticism beyond a declaration in favour of a work, or against it. The only remarks on my work, besides calling it some names, are, that my title is quite wrong, ' because I have not given an account of the religion of the Protestants in Germany, (which may easily be far better than that of the English Episcopal Church,) nor of the state of the Protestant Church in Germany, (which has forms and aims far more favourable to religious truth than the Episcopal Church, which is dependent on stiff and spirit-killing forms,) but merely of the theology, of certain Protestant writers.' The writer moreover then says, that ' I was not long enough in Germany to ob-

serve accurately'—I never pretended to do so,—
that 'German travellers in England have told me
a great deal'—I never saw one before my work
was printed,—and that 'I ought to read many
more German books, and gain a wider knowledge
of German literature.' The last recommendation
I shall be most happy to take, though not exactly in the sense it is offered. I have read
enough now, and too much of Rationalist divinity,
and am wearied with violence, and rashness, and
self-will, and ignorance.

In the second article there is only a very short
analysis of Dr. Bretschneider's work, a commendation of his fourfold division of German theology, and of his temper (!), and a recommendation to translate his work into English.

www.ingramcontent.com/pod-product-compliance
Lightning Source LLC
LaVergne TN
LVHW081353060426
835510LV00013B/1805